THE OXFOR

HARMONY

VOLUME ONE

£1.20
Net

THE OXFORD HARMONY

VOLUME ONE

by

R. O. MORRIS

M.A., D.Mus. (Oxon.), F.R.C.M.

London
OXFORD UNIVERSITY PRESS
New York   Toronto

Oxford University Press, Ely House, London W. 1

GLASGOW NEW YORK TORONTO MELBOURNE WELLINGTON
CAPE TOWN IBADAN NAIROBI DAR ES SALAAM LUSAKA ADDIS ABABA
DELHI BOMBAY CALCUTTA MADRAS KARACHI LAHORE DACCA
KUALA LUMPUR SINGAPORE HONG KONG TOKYO

ISBN 0 19 317315 8

First edition 1946
Ninth impression 1974

Printed in Great Britain

CONTENTS

VOLUME ONE

CONTENTS

INTRODUCTION TO VOLUME ONE

THE first volume of *The Oxford Harmony* deals only with diatonic harmony and the common methods of ornamentation, leaving all the chromatic chords, and the preliminary stages of applied harmony, to be expounded in Volume II.

The form of this volume differs from that of other manuals covering the same ground, in that three-part work only is recommended as the first course of study. The only serious objection I have heard raised to this plan is that three-part chords are necessarily incomplete.

This objection seems to me invalid. In the first place, the common chord in all its positions is a three-note chord, of which one note has to be doubled in four-part writing. As such, it cannot reasonably be considered incomplete in three parts. By doubling a note or notes in four-, five-, and six-part work, a fuller volume of sound is naturally obtained; but that is a different matter altogether. The chords of the seventh are in rather a different position; they are basically four-note chords, of which one note has necessarily to be omitted in three-part writing. But even in four-part work the fifth, in practice, is very commonly omitted and the root doubled, without any objection being raised. Provided the root, the third, and the seventh itself are present, any chord of the seventh is clearly recognizable, both by eye and ear, for what it is, and so may be employed with perfectly good effect in a three-part progression.

None the less, if harmony consisted only of essential notes moving uniformly together (as in the very earliest stages it does), then there would indeed be a very strong case for the four-part view. But if the study is to be made at all attractive, then it is most desirable that the texture should be diversified as soon as possible by the use of the unessential, in the form of passing notes, auxiliary notes, suspensions, and what you will. From an exclusively harmonic point of view these things may be, as their name implies, 'unessential'; but to rhythm they are vital, for without them no variety of rhythm is possible, and without such variety both melody and harmony alike will remain dull and lifeless.

There is no question in my mind that these most essential 'unessentials' may to begin with be more advantageously studied in three parts than in four. In the first place, three parts have much more manœuvring space than four; they can move about freely without getting in each others' way. In the second, it is much more easy for a beginner to keep them all 'under his eye', and so avoid prohibited consecutives and other faulty progressions. Every teacher knows how the casualty list multiplies as soon as unessential notes are introduced by the green hand into his four-part work. By concentrating first of all on three parts only, such casualties may be reduced to a minimum. And finally it may be claimed—I should certainly make the claim myself—that the economy and clarity of style imposed by the limits of three-part harmony is itself a valuable discipline.

There may well be a difference of opinion, however, even among those who are so far in agreement, as to when the transition from three- to four-part work may most advantageously be made. My own view is that Part I should be completed before Part II is tackled. Others may go to the opposite extreme and work chapter by chapter—i.e. chapter ii followed by chapter xvi, then chapter iii followed by chapter xvii, and so on. It is also possible to take a middle course and work first of all, say, as far as the end of chapter vi, and then go on to the corresponding chapters of Part II (i.e. chapters xvi to xx), before returning to complete the rest of Part I. And finally, those who are unwilling to give the three-part system a trial at all are not thereby precluded from using the book. They can take the related chapters in pairs (chapter ii and chapter xvi, and so on), and then work the exercises in four parts only, when the text of both chapters has been assimilated.

There is a doubt in many minds whether the traditional method of teaching this subject by the actual working of harmony and counterpoint exercises is the best that can be devised, and whether some quite different angle of approach might not be preferable.

This is a matter of individual conviction, in which one can only speak for oneself. My own view is that the traditional method is still far the best *for those who can take advantage of it*. It is a form of precision work in which habits of clear and orderly thinking simply have to be formed if any measure of success is to be attained. This discipline is of primary value, with far-reaching effects on the mental development of those who bring to it the necessary concentration. And it may be accepted in music, as in other arts and crafts, that a practical apprenticeship is the surest way to become familiar with the tools of the trade and the right manner of using them.

For such apprenticeship, however, a certain minimum aptitude is prerequisite. There *must* be a certain degree of aural awareness and responsiveness. At the very least, before embarking on a course of practical harmony and counterpoint, the student should be able by ear to recognize and name any interval without hesitation, whether the notes are sounded simultaneously or in succession, and to distinguish between the different positions and inversions of both major and minor common chords sounded in three parts. Anyone who is so far qualified will find that this power of aural recognition can be extensively developed, and that the higher faculty of 'hearing what one sees', and perhaps even the rarer one of 'seeing what one hears' will also unfold by degrees. The judicious use of the pianoforte for testing purposes will greatly assist the development of this inward hearing.

It is a fact, however, that a large number of the music students in our schools and colleges—it may even be a majority of them—do not possess, and prove themselves to be quite incapable of acquiring, the minimum aural requirements postulated above. For them, in my opinion, it is an utter waste of time to work harmony and counterpoint exercises on paper, for they cannot possibly hear what they write. Some other means ought to be devised for giving them such limited theoretical knowledge as may be considered advisable and possible for them to acquire.

R.O.M.

Summer, 1945

Chapter One

PRELIMINARY EXPLANATIONS AND DEFINITIONS

A. INTERVALS

B. CADENCE

C. COMPASS

D. MISCELLANEOUS DEFINITIONS

A. Intervals

HARMONY is concerned with chords, and every chord is a combination of intervals sounded simultaneously. Any systematic study of harmony must therefore begin with an examination of *intervals*. The intervals that form the basis of our Western music, and their measurements in terms of a semitone are as follows:

(1)	Minor Second	contains	1	semitone
(2)	Major Second	,,	2	semitones
(3)	Minor Third	,,	3	,,
(4)	Major Third	,,	4	,,
(5)	Perfect Fourth	,,	5	,,
(6)	Augmented Fourth	,,	6	,,
(7)	Diminished Fifth	,,	6	,,
(8)	Perfect Fifth	,,	7	,,
(9)	Minor Sixth	,,	8	,,
(10)	Major Sixth	,,	9	,,
(11)	Minor Seventh	,,	10	,,
(12)	Major Seventh	,,	11	,,
(13)	Octave	,,	12	,,

Of the above, the octave and the perfect fifth are classified as perfect consonances. The thirds and sixths, both major and minor, are imperfect consonances. The seconds and sevenths, both major and minor, are dissonances.

The perfect fourth, the augmented fourth and the diminished fifth are ambiguous in character.[1] In practice they are treated as dissonances when the bass forms the lower note. But when they occur between two of the *upper* constituent notes of a chord, they rank as consonances, inasmuch as they require no prescribed method of resolution, as do the authentic dissonances.

The augmented fourth and diminished fifth are included in the above

[1] Theoretically, the perfect fourth is *per se* consonant; the augmented fourth and diminished fifth are both dissonant. But throughout this book we shall be concerned with practice rather than theory.

list because they may be diatonic intervals formed between the fourth of the scale and the leading note or vice versa. In addition to these, the perfect fifth, the major second, and the major sixth may be augmented by raising the upper or lowering the lower note chromatically. Similarly the minor third, perfect fourth, minor sixth and minor seventh may be diminished by lowering the upper note or raising the lower note chromatically. These are the only augmentations and diminutions used in practice. Others exist in theory; but only the paradoxically-minded need spend any time in considering, for example, just what kind of a second is formed by the interval B♯—C♭.

The unison is the most perfect of all consonances, but there seems no good reason to follow the usual practice of including it in the list of intervals. Its very name implies that there is *no* interval between the two sounds which form it.

Any of the intervals listed above becomes what is known as a *compound* interval if the upper note is raised or the lower note lowered an octave, or both. This does not alter its character in any way, and the distinction between simple and compound intervals will, for the most part, therefore, be ignored in this treatise. Take, for example, a triad spaced in various ways, as follows:

In the above the B would in each case be described as the third of the chord, D as the fifth, although B is, strictly speaking, the tenth in (2) and (3), while D is actually the twelfth in (2).

Before passing on to our next topic it may be added that any chord which contains no dissonant interval is a concord, any chord which does contain a dissonant interval is a discord. The ambiguous nature of certain intervals (set forth above) will explain how it is, for example, that a diminished triad in root position is a discord, its first inversion a concord, and its second inversion once more a discord. It all depends on the position in the chord of the augmented fourth or diminished fifth:

B. Cadence

The function of cadence in music is, broadly speaking, identical with that of punctuation in literature. It is not enough to say, for example, that a full close (or 'perfect cadence') consists of a progression from dominant to tonic, both chords being in root position. A full close is necessarily such a progression, but such a progression is not necessarily a full close. It would only be so described in a position where it is unmistakably felt as marking the close of a musical phrase or sentence.[1] It is the musical equivalent of a full stop. So is the Plagal Cadence, in which the bass moves from subdominant to tonic. In the Imperfect Cadence (or 'Half-Close'), the progression is to the dominant chord. The chord of approach, if in root position, may be tonic, subdominant, or submediant, or supertonic if the key be major; but it need not necessarily be a chord in root position at all. In the so-called 'Interrupted Cadence' (whose cadential value is really very limited) the progression in the bass is from dominant to submediant, both chords being in root position—i.e. with the fundamental note of the chord in the base. Subjoined are examples of these types of cadence in various major and minor keys:

Perfect Cadences:

Plagal Cadences:

Imperfect Cadences:

[1] These terms, once more, are extraordinarily hard to define except by analogy with the clauses, sentences, periods, and so forth, of written language. Full discussion of this matter here and now would delay us unduly; the reader must be referred to Grove's *Dictionary*, or to the present author's *The Structure of Music*, ch. ii.

With reference to the above, it is worth while pointing out that even in these, the simplest of all harmonic progressions, it is often expedient or necessary to omit the fifth from one or even both chords. The reasons for this will become evident when the student comes to consider the rules of procedure set forth in the next chapter.

C. *Compass of Voices*

Throughout this volume the writing is to be conceived as *vocal* in character—i.e. such as could be sung by normal voices unaccompanied, without undue difficulty in keeping in tune and maintaining the pitch. The first essential, therefore, is to know the compass of the principal types of voice. These, for present purposes, may be taken as follows:

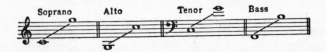

Many individual voices in each category, of course, can exceed the range; but it is best for the beginner to keep within safe limits, and as long as he is working in three parts, at any rate, he will seldom or never want to use the extremes of the possible compass. He should always know exactly what combination of voices he is writing for. SAB and STB are to be avoided on account of the unduly wide spacing that might be entailed (see next chapter for instructions on this point). SAT and ATB will in general be found the most convenient combinations, with SSA and TTB as occasional variants.

D. *Some Miscellaneous Definitions and Elucidations*

(1) In future, instead of saying, 'The triad formed on the tonic (supertonic, mediant, etc.) of the scale', we shall refer to these chords simply by their position in the ascending scale indicated by Roman numerals—i.e. as I, II, III, etc. This will save a good deal of circumlocution.

(2) Conjunct movement means movement by step of a tone or semi-tone; disjunct, movement by leap of a minor third or any larger interval.

(3) Similar and contrary movement mean movement in the same direc-

8

tion and movement in opposite directions respectively. When one part holds or repeats the same note whilst the other part moves, the movement is described as oblique.

(4) In duple time, the first beat is 'strong', the second 'weak'. In quadruple time, first and third are strong, second and fourth weak. In triple time, the second beat is weak in relation to the first but strong in relation to the third, which is thus weak in relation to both the others.

(5) The 'related keys' of any given key are as follows:

Of a major key, IV major and V major; II, III and VI minor.

Of a minor key, IV and V minor, III, VI and VII major (the *descending* form of the melodic minor must be used in making this calculation).

(6) 'Figured Bass' is an old system of musical shorthand based on the position of the upper notes of a chord in relation to its bass, these positions being indicated by small numbers. In this system compound intervals are ignored, with the exception of the ninth, which is usually indicated by 9 rather than by 2.

The notation of each chord in this system will be explained step by step in each successive chapter. In this way all students should gradually be able to master the essentials of the notation, which is historically important and often of great practical convenience as well.

(7) False Relation is the kind of chromatic contradiction that is produced by sounding, for instance, the notes F and F sharp simultaneously (or in immediate juxtaposition) in two different voices.

(8) Sequence means the repetition of a melodic or harmonic figure in a new position of the scale, commonly one step higher or lower.

In a 'diatonic' or 'tonal' sequence, there is no modulation and the correspondence of the intervals is not exact, major being often answered by minor and *vice versa,* e.g. in 'Send him victorious, happy and glorious'.

In a chromatic or 'real' sequence the correspondence of the intervals is exact, so that the repetition of the figure takes place each time in a new key.

Chapter Two

COMMON CHORDS (OR 'TRIADS') IN ROOT POSITION (MAJOR KEYS ONLY)

THIS chapter is in some ways the most important in the book, because its function is to enunciate and explain certain fundamental principles and rules of procedure which apply no less to all the other chapters. These may be classified under three main headings, of which C is the most complex:

A. SPACING

B. DOUBLING AND OMISSION OF NOTES

C. MUTUAL RELATIONSHIP OF CHORDS IN PROGRESSION

A. Spacing

Let us begin by repeating that a common chord consists of a fundamental note (known as the 'root' of the chord) in the bass, together with the third and fifth notes above it. A major scale gives us six such chords— I, II, III, IV, V, and VI. Of these I, IV, and V are known as 'primary' triads, and all of them are 'major'—i.e. the third from the bass is a major third. II, III, and VI are 'secondary' triads, and all of them are 'minor'. VII is not available, for the fifth note is a diminished (or 'false') fifth from the root and the chord is therefore a discord. (Its first inversion, as we have already seen and shall see again, is not.)

Any of these chords may be spaced out in various ways. In trying to decide which of these are *per se* good and which bad (irrespective of their relation to any possible preceding and following chords) bear three points in mind:

(1) Each note must lie comfortably within the compass of the type of voice that has to sing it.

(2) The outer parts should be kept within a reasonable distance from one another. In three-part writing, two octaves is about the limit, with two octaves and a third as the maximum possible extension in case of emergency.

(3) Avoid wide gaps as far as possible. As will be seen later, however, the exigencies of part-writing will often make such avoidance impossible. In that event it is better for a wide gap to lie between the two lower than the two upper voices. A tenth may be taken as the normal limit between the two lower voices, and an octave between the two upper ones.

Here are some thoroughly bad spacings of the tonic chord of C Major:

Say exactly what is wrong with each and then (having found out in this way how not to do it) space out for yourself a number of similar chords on various degrees of various major scales, in what you consider a satisfactory manner, varying the vocal combinations and the disposition of the chords as much as you can within the limits laid down.

B. Doubling and Omission

Considerations of correct part-writing, it has already been explained, will frequently necessitate the omission of one note of a triad and the doubling of another in place of it. The note to be omitted, in such a case, is the fifth. The note doubled may be either the root or the third, *provided the third does not happen to be the leading note of the key*. That is a most important proviso, whose urgency cannot be too strongly impressed upon the student from the very beginning. Never double the leading note of any key in which you may find yourself, whether tonic or otherwise. At a cadence, especially, its progression is not free, and the result of doubling it will be either the perpetration of consecutive octaves (see next section), or their unskilful avoidance. Even in non-cadential places, when the leading note does not necessarily rise to the tonic, the doubling sounds awkward and is to be sternly discountenanced. The doubling of any major third note in a triad is frowned upon in certain academic quarters, but this is mere prejudice. In some situations such doubling is imperative, and all the great composers from Palestrina onwards have made use of it without compunction whenever the natural progression of the parts made it convenient. This is not to say that the doubling of a major third need be or should be used indiscriminately.

As regards the omission of notes, the third should never be left out of a triad except occasionally from the opening or final chord, which may be a combination of octave and unison. In a three-part perfect cadence, the progression of the voices every now and again makes this the most convenient form of close.

Here are a few examples of such doublings (both at the octave and unison) and omissions, which the observant reader may already have noticed in many of the chords forming the specimen cadences given on pp. 7 and 8:

As it is just as necessary to be able to think downwards from a melody as upwards from a bass, it would be just as well for the student, before going further, to complete suitable chords to the following notes, in the appropriate keys, each given note being regarded as the top note of its chords. The bass, at this stage, can only be an octave, a third, or a fifth (simple or more probably compound) below the given note, so that it ought to be practically impossible for him—or her—to go very far wrong. It will be found that any of the three—third, fifth or octave—will form a suitable bass, and these various alternatives should all be worked out.

Remember that after the bass note has been fixed, the third note will be a third, a fifth, or octave, as the case may be, *from the bass*, not from the treble. Painful experience has convinced me that this warning is not superfluous.

Complete the triads of which the following are the upper notes:

C. Mutual Relationship of Chords in Progression

The first question to be discussed under this heading is that of 'prohibited consecutives'. The reason for these prohibitions is matter for speculation and discussion between instructor and pupil. It is a most interesting question, but space forbids us to enter into it here and now. We shall just accept the prohibitions at their face value, as one of the generally received conventions of 'classical' music.

The intervals concerned are, in the first place, the unison, the octave and the perfect fifth. None of these may be taken successively on two different notes between the same two voices, either by similar or contrary movement. Nor may a unison be followed immediately by an octave, or vice versa. Repetition of the *same* octave or fifth, however, is not regarded as a breach of this rule. The following will make the exact meaning of all this clear at a glance:

Moreover, it is better not to approach a fifth or octave by similar motion at all (at any rate between the outer voices) unless one of the two parts concerned, preferably the upper, moves by step:

[It may be said here, in anticipation of later chapters, that the above rule, so far as fifths are concerned, does not apply when moving from one arrangement or position to another of *the same chord*. And (again in anticipation) consecutive fifths of which one is diminished are permitted between the upper parts, but not between one of the upper parts and the bass.]

An exception is made in the case (as below) of triads in root position when the base falls a fifth and either of the upper parts falls from the third of the first chord to the fifth of the second:

Such progressions are often described as 'hidden consecutives'. 'Implied consecutives' would more accurately define the nature of the objection.

It will be noticed that in the great majority of the above examples, the consecutives lie between one of the upper parts and the bass. This is simply because, when using only three-part triads in root position, it is difficult if not impossible to make the upper parts progress in such fashion. As soon as the student comes to use inverted chords (ch. iv), he will find that they are just as likely to occur between the upper voices. It is to be hoped he will remember that they are no less reprehensible in that position.

One should not approach or quit a unison by similar motion (a and b below) unless absolutely compelled, as one occasionally is. And overlapping progressions like c and d are also to be avoided:

COMMON CHORDS IN ROOT POSITION

Before going any further, it would be as well for the student to practise writing a few cadences similar to the specimens exhibited on p. 7. Various keys are to be chosen and the spacing and distribution of the voices varied as far as possible within the prescribed limits. It must be remembered that in the perfect and 'interrupted' cadence the leading note should rise to the tonic. It follows that when writing a perfect cadence for three voices the fifth has to be omitted from the tonic chord.

With the present very limited material it is not possible to provide exercises or examples of any great length. Short groups of from three to six chords are about all that can be attempted. Discussion of the general characteristics of good melodic writing is therefore deferred until ch. iv (see p. 24). If the student cares to read that section in advance before working the exercises at the end of this chapter, so much the better; but he should be able to manage well enough for the time being if he avoids wide leaps and makes his voices move, to the best of his ability, in the same sort of way as those of the specimen workings.

The student of harmony must, from the very beginning, learn to rely on his ear to tell him what progressions sound right and what sound wrong. The ear is the judge; the 'rules' merely codify, in general terms, the judgements of the ear. It may be of help, nevertheless, in this opening stage, to have a few general observations as to the conduct of the bass, for if the bass is ill-chosen, the entire harmonic structure will be faulty. The following maxims will be found worth bearing in mind:

(1) Roots a fourth or fifth apart, whether rising or falling, are generally good.

(2) Roots a third apart are also, in the main, satisfactory, but roots falling a third are preferable to roots rising a third. In the latter case it is better for the second chord (the higher of the two roots) to bear the stronger accent.

(3) Roots lying a tone or semitone apart need some care. Rising a tone, especially IV to V or V to VI, they are good. The exception is III, which is a bad neighbour both to IV and II. For the time being it is safer to place III only in juxtaposition with roots having one or more notes in common with it, that is to say, with I, V or VI. Roots falling a second are not so good as roots rising a second. They are best in effect when the outer parts move by contrary motion. Of the available progressions of this kind, VI to V is the best. II to I is only fair, and V to IV is apt to sound unsatisfactory. In three-part writing, especially, it is best avoided by the beginner.

Here are some specimens of short groups of triads, so arranged as to end in every case with one of the cadences already classified:

[In the following exercises a suitable combination of voices is indicated in each case. After this chapter, the student will be left to use his own judgement in this matter.]

Add two parts above:

Add two parts below:

Figuring. The figuring of a triad is, strictly speaking, $\frac{5}{3}$ to show that the notes required to complete the chord are the third and fifth from the bass. But in practice, these figures are usually omitted. When a bass note—other than a passing note—was left unfigured, it was understood that that note was to be harmonized as a triad.

Chapter Three

COMMON CHORDS (CONTINUED); MINOR KEYS

THROUGHOUT this book we shall use the melodic in preference to the harmonic form of the minor scale. It is melodically smoother, avoiding as it does the awkward augmented interval between the sixth and seventh degrees; it is harmonically richer, because on certain degrees—II, III, V, and VII—it offers alternative formations which are not available in the harmonic form of the scale.

All that was said in the last chapter about the spacing of chords, the doubling and omission of notes and the prohibition of certain consecutives, applies equally here, and there is really nothing to add under these headings. The further remarks about the general relationship of the roots in the bass are also valid in the main as far as they go, but need some amplification.

Take a particular scale—A minor will do as well as any other—and consider the possible triads that may be formed on its successive degrees:

Of the above, II, IIIA, VIA, and VIIA can all be ruled out for the present, for all are discords. IIIA is an augmented triad whose use as a prepared suspension is illustrated in ch. ix, p. 61. The others are all diminished triads, which the student will seldom find worth using, even when he has acquired the experience that will enable him to use them correctly. But some of the remainder call for comment:

(1) *IIA and IVA*. The fifth note—F sharp—is required to proceed immediately, in the same part, to G sharp. Hence these chords can only be used at present in juxtaposition with VA, the only consonant triad in the scale which contains a G sharp.

(2) *III*. Its most congenial associates are VI and VII. It precedes IV more happily than it follows it and follows I more happily than it precedes it.

(3) *V and VA*. VA, of course, is generally to be preferred, and must always be used in cadential progressions to or from I. V is chiefly useful in association with III or VII.

(4) *VII*. It should never be followed by I; the effect would be that of a cadence which has miscarried. It may conceivably follow I, however, if the bass of the succeeding chord is a note which is more conveniently reached via G natural than by any other route.

Although the note G natural occurs in the *descending* form of A minor,

17

it must not be supposed that its progress, in practice, is necessarily downwards. Very often it is so, but it must be considered free, subject to the normal limitations of melodic procedure (for which see p. 24) to move to any accessible note of the ensuing chord. In itself, however, the note has a stronger affinity with C major, of which it is the dominant, than with A minor. To correct this ambiguity it is desirable, though not essential, to follow it shortly by a chord containing G sharp. The following approach to a half-close, for example, is admirable in effect:

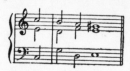

No fear need be felt that the proximity of the G natural and the G sharp in such a context, will create a 'false relationship'.

It was easier to explain all this in terms of a particular key than to expound it in generalities. But the application of these principles to any other minor key is a very simple matter. The student should now form a few cadences for himself in various minor keys, not forgetting to put in the accidental that is now necessary to raise the seventh of the scale when it figures as part of the chord V in the perfect, imperfect and interrupted cadences.

Before he goes on to the more extended exercises below, two additional rules must be given:

(1) Avoid the use, melodically, of any augmented interval. Be specially careful with the progressions IV—V and V—VI.

(2) Any diminished interval that may be used melodically should be followed by step within the interval, e.g.:

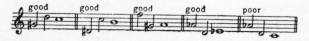

Specimens:

Add two parts above:

Add two parts below:

Figuring. The sign ♯ or ♮, as the case may be, is enough to indicate the raising of the seventh note of the scale to form the leading note at a cadence. It is the third note of the dominant chord, and any accidental sign with no figure beside it was understood as affecting the third note from the bass.

In a perfect or plagal cadence, the third of the final tonic chord may also be made major if so preferred (the so-called 'Tierce de Picardie'). This also has to be indicated, in figured bass notation, by the sign ♯ or ♮, as the case may be. Some of the specimens above have purposely been so figured by way of example. The student is strongly advised to figure all his completed workings from now onwards; if he does, he will find that he acquires complete understanding of this time-honoured musical shorthand with very little trouble.

FIRST INVERSIONS OF THE COMMON CHORD (KNOWN ALSO AS 'CHORDS OF THE SIXTH')

IN the first inversion of a triad, the root of the chord becomes one of the upper notes, and the third takes its place as the bass of the new position. As before, the upper notes may be distributed in various ways, and as regards the spacing, precisely the same principles apply. And, once more, it is sometimes convenient to omit one note and double one of the others. Obviously you cannot leave out the sixth, otherwise the chord would not be clearly recognizable for what it is. Therefore the third of the chord (the fifth of the triad in its root position) has to be omitted. Either of the other notes may then be doubled, but in three-part writing it is preferable (other things being equal) to double the sixth.

Here are some typical lay-outs of the first inversion of the chord of C major:

Before going further, it may be as well to remind the student that although a diminished triad in root position is dissonant, its first inversion is, for all practical purposes, consonant. Therefore the inversion of the leading triad (VII) in the major key may be freely used. In the minor scale, the alternative forms of II and VII likewise come into consideration. Look at the following (the key of course is here A minor):

In root position, as we saw in chapter iii, only the forms (b) and (d) were available. The inversions of these may still be used, but so may the inversions of (a) and (c). The F sharp must still rise to G sharp and when it is required to do so, the form (f) will naturally be used. Otherwise, the alternative form (e) should usually be adopted. As between (g) and (h), the choice will depend on circumstances. Very little practice should enable anyone with a normally perceptive ear to select the right alternative for any particular case. In future, when reference is made to the first inversions of II and VII in the minor key, it may be taken that (e) and (g) are indicated, not (f) and (h), unless expressly specified.

Chords of the sixth, generally speaking, are excellent for mixing purposes. With their aid, it is incomparably easier to find a suitable harmonization for a given melody or bass than when triads only are employed. Let us consider them first in relation to cadence, and see what new possibilities they offer.

(1) The first inversion of VII gives a new form of final cadence. A bass that ends by falling a step on to the tonic note should always be so harmonized, and the resulting cadence, though less conclusive than a full close, makes quite a satisfactory ending to a short sentence or period, either in a major or a minor key:

(2) The first inversion of V gives a modified version of the perfect cadence, also quite acceptable within limits (one would not end a symphony so):

(3) First inversions of I, II and IV all make good chords of approach to V at a half-close:

FIRST INVERSIONS OF COMMON CHORD

It would be a feasible though laborious task to tabulate all the triads and their inversions and indicate the various degrees of compatibility or incompatibility existing between each pair. To do so, however, would be superfluous and undesirable, for any student who required the help of such a list in order to write reasonably correct and euphonious harmony would be far better employed in some other way. The ear, aided at discretion by the use of the piano for testing, is the proper guide as to what sounds right and what does not.

After studying the specimens above, it should now be possible to complete the short phrases below without undue difficulty. Perhaps a word of advice about repeated notes may be timely. When these are in the bass, it is usually best to harmonize one as $\frac{5}{3}$, the other as $\frac{6}{3}$, or vice versa. But a change from one position to another of a $\frac{5}{3}$ chord is also quite good, provided the first of the repeated notes bears a stronger accent than the second. If the second of the repeated notes is the first note of a new phrase, there is no objection to repeating the chord exactly as it was before, if convenient. This holds good for repeated notes in the melody likewise, but in any other position repeated melody notes usually demand a change of chord.

Of the following phrases, the first four of each set are in major keys, the other four in minor:

Add 2 parts above:

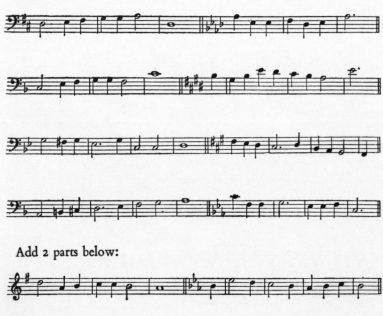

Add 2 parts below:

The exercises which will follow are rather longer and subdivide into two or more phrases, each of which should terminate with some sort of cadence, intermediate or final as the case may be. In this set the phrase-marks have been added to facilitate the harmonization; but in future the student will be left to do his own phrasing. This he should do in every exercise, be it melody or bass, before starting to add the other parts.

A few additional hints as to the best method of working the exercises may not be out of place. Let us suppose, first of all, that he is working from a given bass.

The first thing is to add the melody. This is of prime importance, and even within the limits of these short exercises it is the student's first business to make it easily singable and reasonably attractive. It may be instructive to show three workings of the same bass:

The first two, in their different ways, are both about as bad as they can be, the sluggish, constipated immobility of (a) being no more commendable than the kangaroo-like leaps and bounds of (b), although the actual choice of chords, as chords, is not bad in either case. (c) is a tolerably good working.

fIRST INVERSIONS OF COMMON CHORD

Beginners at this stage of melody-making will be well advised to impose upon themselves the following restraints:

(1) Do not have too much disjunct movement. Use it as a necessary foil to stepwise movement, but use it with discretion.

(2) Two or (at most) three leaps may occasionally be taken in the same direction, provided their combined range does not exceed an octave.

(3) The largest single leap that may be taken is that of an octave, and the leap of a minor sixth or any larger interval should be preceded and followed by notes within the compass of that interval.

(4) Advice regarding the use of augmented and diminished intervals has already been given (see ch. iii, p. 18).

(5) No one type of movement—similar, contrary or oblique—should prevail for too long at a time between the melody and the bass. Four chords is about the limit.

(6) A judicious but sparing use of repeated notes helps to solidify the melodic structure. Repeated notes should for choice be differently harmonized, especially if the first of them comes on a weak accent.

Now let us imagine, for a change, that the melody is given. What is the next step?

The answer is: Add the bass; but many students find at first—and some always—that this is more easily said than done. If you are not one of the lucky ones to whom any simple melody immediately suggests an appropriate bass and harmony, the safest way to begin is to make up your mind what cadences come where, fill those in first, and then work backwards a chord at a time till it is completed. Then survey it as a whole and make sure it conforms, in the main, to the six guiding principles enunciated above, for all these—except to some extent the first—apply equally to every part. The function of a bass is not the same as that of a melody, but both alike—and for that matter the middle part as well—must exhibit a certain orderliness and shapeliness of contour. And that is what the six points above set forth will help to ensure.

Just one caution about the middle part: If this moves in a sequence of parallel sixths with the bass, it is likely to find itself moving also in parallel fifths with the melody.

Of the exercises below, once more, the first four of each set are in major keys, the other four minor.

Add two parts above:

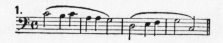

Add two parts below:

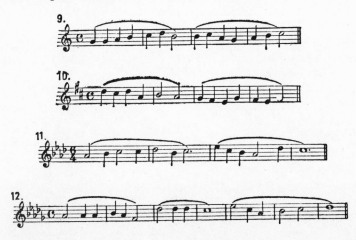

Figuring. The full figuring of a chord of the sixth is $^6_3$, but in practice the figure 6 alone is normally sufficient. If the third (in a minor key for example) needs to be altered chromatically, then the figuring will be $^6_\sharp$ or $^6_\flat$ or $^6_\natural$.

Chapter Five

A. UNACCENTED PASSING NOTES (DIATONIC)
B. UNACCENTED AUXILIARY NOTES
C. SUBSIDIARY HARMONY NOTES

A. *Unaccented Passing Notes (Diatonic)*

A DIATONIC passing note is an unessential note inserted between two essential notes lying a third apart. It may be, and usually is, dissonant with the bass. In the third of the examples below, the note B, though actually consonant with the bass, is considered 'dissonant by position', as the harmony of the beat is the chord of D minor, of which B is not a constituent note. It will be noticed that if the beat is simple, the passing note may be either a half or a quarter of the beat value (a b c and e below); if the beat is compound, it is sometimes a third (d), but more often a sixth, as in f (though the quavers marked + might be regarded as subsidiary beats):

Single passing notes are always most effective when they lead from a weak to a strong beat as in (a) (b) and (c) above. Passing notes between strong and weak beats are by no means forbidden, but it is often better in such cases to follow up with another passing or auxiliary note in the same voice between the weak beat and the following strong beat, as in (d) above, or to precede in a similar way, as in (e).

Passing and other unessential notes add enormously to the rhythmic interest and variety of music, but the beginner will find that the danger of forbidden consecutives is increased by their employment, for though such notes may create fifths or octaves, they cannot 'save' them. He may think this very unfair, but there it is; the following, for example, are all incorrect. An example of 'hidden' consecutives (d) is included, for these too come to a certain extent under the ban, the rule being, in effect, that the note in question must be approached by step *from an essential note*:

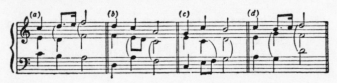

Passing notes may be doubled in thirds or sixths, while the octave may also be doubled as a passing note by conjunct and contrary movement. Such notes should be of the same value, half, third, or quarter beats as the case may be; the use of passing notes of different time-values simultaneously is apt to create a momentary harmonic confusion, and should be rigorously eschewed until the study of combined counterpoint has shown how such confusion may be avoided.

The examples below show the right and wrong ways of doing it:

When using passing notes, care should be taken to avoid quitting the interval of a second by similar motion (a and b below). The simplest solution, very often, is to double the passing note (c), but example (b) is not amenable to this correction and the passing note should be omitted or the passage rewritten. As regards the ninth, one need not be so particular, and there is no real objection to (d); but even so the doubling of the passing note is to be preferred when feasible (e):

Before passing on to the subject of auxiliary and subsidiary notes, it may be as well to have a little preliminary practice in handling passing notes by themselves, after first looking carefully at the two specimens below:

In the following exercises, all passing notes are indicated by slurs, and all notes not slurred are to be regarded as essential. In future exercises, the student will often be left to decide for himself which notes are essential and which are not.

Add two parts above:

Add two parts below:

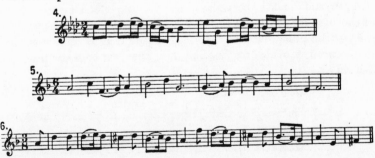

29

B. *Unaccented Auxiliary Notes*

An auxiliary note is similar in status to a passing note, but instead of passing forward to the note a third away from the principal note, it moves back—upwards or downwards as the case may be—to the note it started from:

The sharp in brackets is to indicate that when the auxiliary lies a major second below the principal note, it may be raised chromatically at will, so that the major second becomes a minor. Such alteration is frequently desirable, but only the ear can decide when and when not to do it. There is no rule of thumb.

Single auxiliary notes, like passing notes (but even more so), are more effective between a weak and a strong beat than vice versa. They need not be used singly, however; the effect is admirable when the principal note is preceded or followed by a passing note in the manner shown below:

Note the conformation of these four-note groups carefully. In the first four of them the first note comes on a weak beat; the four notes are really two pairs and should be harmonized as such—i.e. preferably with a change of chord. In the others, the first note marks a strong beat; two chords are still quite in order, but the group may equally well be harmonized by a single chord, provided the first and third notes are both constituents of that chord:

If the beat is compound, the first note will be a dotted note,[1] crotchet or quaver as the case may be, according to the value of the beat; otherwise precisely the same principle applies:

A word of caution may be uttered in regard to the iteration of auxiliaries in figures like these:

In actual composition, such figures, treated thematically, can be most effective; one need only think of such things as the openings of the over-ture to 'Figaro' and of Brahms's G major sextet, or the principal episode in the finale of Bach's organ sonata in C major, or the ending of the main subject from Purcell's charming little rondo in the 'Fairy Queen':

But in short exercises of an elementary character such iteration is apt to produce a faintly ridiculous effect, and a combination of auxiliary and passing notes, as previously exemplified, is to be preferred. Regarding the third of the figures (c) shown in the last example but one, note that the effect here is not one of iterated auxiliaries at all, but of two independent passing note groups. It is all a question of rhythm; both melodically and harmonically, what is ineffective with one accentuation may be admirable with another.

Auxiliaries, like passing notes, may be doubled in thirds or sixths. In this connexion, observe that if one of the auxiliaries is raised chromatically in the manner recommended above (p. 30), the other must also be so

[1] The dot has gate-crashed into the party. It should not, properly speaking, have made its appearance till chapter viii, where its harmonic function is explained. Never mind. No harm will be done if the student will remember that for the time being alike in simple and compound beats, no change of harmony is required 'on the dot'. In other words, a dotted note and the short note following it will be marked with a slur, to indicate that there is to be no change of chord during this process.

raised unless it is already a semitone (not a full tone) below its principal note. Of the following, (a) (c) and (d) are all good, (b) is bad:

Before proceeding to consider the use of subsidiary harmony notes, a little practice in the art of combining passing and auxiliary notes is to be recommended. Specimens:

Add two parts above:

Add two parts below:

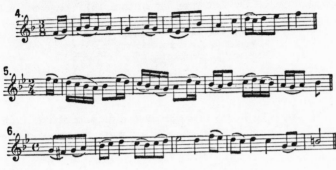

C. Subsidiary Harmony Notes

A subsidiary note is just as much a part of the harmony as the principal note; it is only called subsidiary because it is unaccented, or less strongly accented. It may itself be of full beat value, e.g.:

Beat notes of this nature, however, should not be so treated in the present series of exercises if unslurred; they should be given a different chord, as hitherto.

What we are more concerned with in this chapter is subsidiary notes of smaller value, especially when used in combination with passing and auxiliary notes. Before considering these more complex patterns, however, it seems advisable to emphasize a few points in connexion with subsidiaries as such, for there is a right and wrong way of using these notes. In particular:

(1) Like passing and auxiliary notes, single subsidiary notes are more happily placed between a weak beat and a strong than vice versa. (No apology is made for stressing once more the great importance of this matter of accentuation as an element in melodic and harmonic structure.)

(2) The fundamental proprieties of melodic formation must always be borne in mind, for these apply to subsidiary no less than to principal notes. E.g. if there is a wide jump—say of a sixth or octave—to or from a subsidiary, both approach and departure should be from within the interval.

(3) If subsidiaries are used in successive beats, care must be taken to

33

avoid an arpeggio-like formation characteristic of pianoforte rather than of vocal writing. Of the following, for instance, (b) is preferable to (a):

(4) The increased danger of consecutive fifths and octaves must be borne in mind (a), and formations which involve the use of such consecutives on successive beats (b) are discouraged by most examiners:

(5) Subsidiaries in the bass should be used sparingly and with great caution. Those a fourth below or fifth above the bass are apt to suggest an ambiguous use of the $\frac{6}{4}$ chord (see next chapter), as illustrated by (a) and (b) hereunder. If the harmony is a triad, the subsidiary lying a third above the bass is generally safe (c); if a chord of the sixth, that lying a third below it (d):

Subsidiary notes appear to most advantage when used in combination with passing and auxiliary notes to form melodic patterns such as these:

After digesting what has been said above, the student should find no difficulty in finding suitable and correct harmonic treatment for such patterns. There is just one more point to be dealt with, and that is the use of subsidiary and passing (or auxiliary) notes simultaneously in different voices. This is perfectly feasible, provided such notes are consonant with one another, e.g.:

Specimens:

Add two parts above:

Add two parts below:

Figuring. For passing and auxiliary notes in the bass itself a short line is used. Groups in which unessential and subsidiary notes are combined with no change of harmony are also indicated by a line underneath the group indicated. Passing notes in the upper voices are not indicated by figuring unless it is expressly desired that a particular progression—87, for example, or 65—should be employed in one of those voices.

The specimen exercises in this chapter have been figured, and it is hoped that these examples, together with the brief explanation above, will afford a sufficiently clear indication of the procedure commonly employed.

Chapter Six

THE SIX-FOUR CHORD

IN the second inversion of the common chord, the fifth of the original triad becomes the bass, and the third partners the root in the upper story:

Both sixth and fourth are indispensable constituents; therefore, in three-part work, no note can be omitted or doubled, unless subsidiary notes are introduced. With the help of these, as will be seen later, a little judicious faking will often enable one to surmount the limitations inherent in three-part writing.

The three commonly recognized types of six-four chord are:

(A) Passing six-four.
(B) Auxiliary six-four.
(C) Cadential six-four.

To the above another may conveniently be added, viz.:

(D) Appoggiatura six-four.

For the meaning of the term 'appoggiatura', if he does not already know it, the student is referred to chapter xiv.

Let us now consider these four types in their due order:

A. The Passing Six-Four

This is soon dealt with. It requires the doubling of the bass note, so that it is not available for use in three-part writing, as only one voice is left for the no less indispensable fourth and sixth (faking by means of subsidiaries is not practicable in this case). Consideration of it is therefore deferred until chapter xx, and one may add that this is no great loss.

B. The Auxiliary Six-Four

This chord is, in essence, no more than the harmonic decoration of a common chord by means of the two upper auxiliaries doubled in thirds or sixths. It may be devoid of accent (a) or weakly accented (b), or strongly accented (c):

THE SIX-FOUR CHORD

This chord, though not of cardinal importance, has its uses. Any major or minor triad is amenable to this form of decoration except II in the minor scale.

C. The Cadential Six-Four

This is formed on the dominant note of the scale and is thus the second inversion of I. It is, really, only one special example of the type described elsewhere in this chapter as the 'appoggiatura' six-four. But it is used much more often than the other chords of this type, and from the fact that it figures so frequently in perfect, imperfect and 'interrupted' cadences, it has acquired a status of its own, and is generally distinguished by the name 'Cadential'. Here are examples of the kind of way it is used in these various types of cadence, both in the major or minor keys:

The following conditions are laid down for the employment both of this and the other 'appoggiatura' six-four chords (to be exemplified later):

(1) The chord, being in practice a discord, requires 'resolution'. To effect this, the fourth must fall stepwise to the third. The sixth usually (though not invariably) falls in a parallel progression to the fifth, so that the chord of resolution is the triad on the same bass note, which may be either held or repeated. (In the specific case of the 'cadential' six-four, the chord of resolution may equally well be the dominant seventh, provided the cadence is of the perfect or 'interrupted' kind. At a half-close, the triad is to be preferred; the dominant seventh is weak and ineffective, as a rule, in that position.)

(2) The six-four chord should be placed in a stronger accentual position than the chord on which it resolves.

(3) The bass of a six-four must not be approached by leap, except from a triad or diatonic seventh in root position. The diatonic sevenths, of course, do not come into the picture yet, but they will do so presently (chapter xi).

An exception is made in favour of the triad of which any given six-four is the second inversion; it may safely be approached from the first inversion of that triad (as in the third of the examples above).

In the cadential six-four, the fourth may appear as a subsidiary note, whether it is or is not also present as a principal note:

In the former case ([a] above), note that the fourth in the alto, where it is the principal note, has to resolve up a step instead of down a step in order to avoid moving in consecutive octaves with the subsidiary fourth above it. This is a licence justifiable in this particular situation, but not in any other.

[The fourth is never to be doubled *as a principal note*, but in three-part writing the temptation so to double it cannot well arise.]

D. The 'Appoggiatura' Six-Four

It has been explained above that the conditions governing the use of this chord are precisely the same, in all essentials, as those laid down for the 'cadential' six-four. It is obviously unnecessary to recapitulate those conditions, but as these other six-four chords have been somewhat neglected in previous text-books, it seems worth while to review them briefly, taking each degree of the major and minor scale in turn, and illustrating the use of the six-four formed thereon. In the following enumeration the first figure indicates the degree of the scale, the second (in brackets) the triad of which the six-four formed on that degree is an inversion.

I. (IV). Useful chiefly as a means of delaying or prolonging a plagal cadence, or even a perfect one. The latter, however, though simple in four parts, is not so feasible in three, especially in a minor key, where some faking is necessary:

II. (V). In a major key, quite good. If used in the minor the resolution must be to a $\frac{6}{3}$ (the first inversion of VII) instead of the customary $\frac{5}{3}$ (see [b] below). This is in no sense a licence; the sixth is not a dissonant note, and there is no obligation upon it to follow the fourth downwards, although in practice it usually does so. It is at perfect liberty to remain where it is (or rise a third to double the bass note if convenient):

III. (VI). Quite serviceable; but here again it is often better to resolve it on to the $\frac{6}{3}$ rather than the $\frac{5}{3}$. It all depends on what the following chord is to be:

IV. (VII). Possible in major keys, in spite of the fact that this particular six-four, being the second inversion of VII, has an augmented fourth with the bass. In the minor key this can be avoided by using the flattened sixth (the seventh note of the descending melodic minor scale); the chord then makes an admirable effect when approaching a half-close:

V. (I). [This is the 'cadential' six-four, which has already been discussed.]

VI. (II). Admirable in the major keys. In the minor a $\frac{6}{3}$ resolution is often preferable to a $\frac{5}{3}$:

VII. (III). The resolution is necessarily to a chord of the sixth in the major keys. In the minor, when the flattened seventh is used in the bass, the six-four in front of it is quite serviceable, though here once more the $\frac{6}{3}$ resolution may often be more convenient than the $\frac{5}{3}$:

Though these secondary six-fours (as one might term them) are, with the exceptions noted above, eminently satisfactory in their effect when judiciously used, they are not chords to be employed with undue frequency. In the specimens which follow they have been deliberately over-used in order to provide as many examples as possible within a short space of time, and in the subsequent exercises the student should likewise make a point of introducing them wherever possible, for the sake of practice. Let the fourth be in the top part for choice, especially when the resolution is to a chord of the sixth.

Specimens:

Add two parts above:

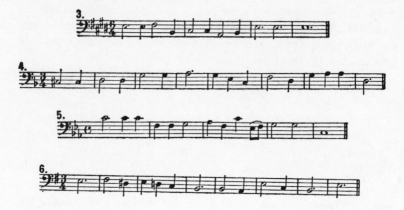

Add two parts below:

Figuring. The chord and its resolution are figured $^{65}_{43}$ or $^{6-}_{43}$, as the case may be.

Chapter Seven

A. THE CHORD OF THE DOMINANT SEVENTH
(Root Position)
B. MODULATION (First Stage)

A

The Chord of the Dominant Seventh (Root Position)

Take the triad of V, add the seventh from the bass on top, and you
have, in its simplest form, the chord of the dominant seventh:

This, it will be seen, is a four-note chord, therefore something has to
be omitted in three-part harmony. The seventh (the characteristic note)
and the third (the leading note) are both essential, so that the fifth is
perforce left out.

Both the fifth and the doubled root, however, can and often do figure
as subsidiary notes:

As this chord contains a dissonant interval (the seventh) it is a discord,
and as such requires resolution. The accepted resolutions of the chord
are two:

(1) The seventh resolves downwards by step, while the bass rises a
fourth or falls a fifth, thus providing a variant of the perfect cadence.

(2) The seventh, as before, resolves down by step, whilst the bass rises
a step, thus providing a variant of the 'interrupted' cadence:

There **is** another possibility—the so-called 'stationary seventh'. In this case the seventh remains where it is, while the other voices both move upwards or (less effectively) downwards a step:

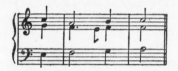

This procedure should only be followed very sparingly; none the less, if used exactly in the right place and at the right time it can be very effective, precisely because it is not just what one is expecting. Its effectiveness varies inversely as its frequency.

The seventh, being a dissonant note, is not to be doubled.

It has already been observed (see p. 30) that this chord may well be associated with the cadential six-four in a perfect or 'interrupted' cadence but not in a half-close.

Figuring. The full figuring is $\frac{7}{5}$, but even in four parts the figure 7 alone is generally considered sufficient.

It is not worth while setting exercises of any length or elaboration for the sole purpose of introducing this one chord. Before going on to the next section, the student should give himself sufficient practice in the correct formation and resolution of the chord by writing cadences involving the use of it in various major and minor keys, preceded by two or three suitable chords, after the manner of the following:

B

Modulation—(The First Stage)

Modulation means, in music, the passing from one key into another. In theory, one cannot be sure that such a transition has been made until both dominant seventh and tonic chords of the new key have been sounded. Take this chord by itself, for example:

Alone, it does not tell us whether we are in C major or C minor, or even in A minor, where the chord might conceivably be used in certain contexts, though not to form a cadence in that key, for which the note G sharp would be required. Followed by the tonic of C major or C minor, however, it leaves no possible doubt that that and no other is the key in which, for the moment, we are. It is obvious, therefore, that the dominant seventh is a decisive element in modulation, and that modulation as a subject could not profitably be discussed until that chord had been explained.

At the same time, it should be recognized that the leading note of itself has such force that an unmistakable modulation may be effected without actually using the chord of the dominant seventh in the new key. Consider the following, for example:

In the above, modulations are made in turn from C major to each of its related keys. Nobody could deny that the cadences in every case are decisive, yet in none of them is a chord of the dominant seventh employed. In the following, the same modulations are once more effected, and this time the dominant seventh figures in each of them, either as principal or as secondary note:

MODULATION

In the following short exercises, therefore, the student is free to follow his own judgement in this matter, but he is advised to use the chord of the seventh enough to familiarize himself with the manner of its employment in the new key. What that key is, he must find out for himself in each case. There is not always an accidental in the given part to guide him, but as each exercise ends with a full close in a new key, it should hardly be possible for him to go astray.

Specimens:

Add two parts above:

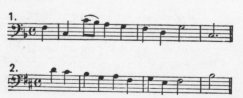

Add two parts below:

By means of modulation, it becomes possible to construct more extensive and highly organized musical sentences than those hitherto attempted.
In these, not every modulation will be an emphatic full close such as con-

cludes the short exercises above. Modulation may quite well be effected by means of an 'inverted' cadence in the new key; that is to say, neither of the chords forming the cadence need be in root position. Sometimes one may be, sometimes neither. The actual possibilities, stated in terms of the bass with reference to the *new* key, are more or less as follows:

(1) Bass moves from VII to I. In this case harmonize with a six-three on VII and pass the sixth down through the flat fifth to the third of I ([a] and [b]). In this way all four notes of the new dominant seventh come into play, and the effect is that of the first inversion of that chord.

(2) Bass moves II to I. Harmonize II as a six-three, or as a triad with a fifth passing up through the sixth to the tonic of I ([c] and [d]). Thus both the seventh and the leading note of the new key come into action and the modulation is free from all ambiguity.

(3) Bass moves V to III (possibly passing down through IV). In this case, of course, III must be a six-three (the first inversion) of I [(e) and [f]] V being its dominant in root position.

(4) Bass moves IV to III. When the inversions of the dominant have been learnt, here is an obvious case for using the last of them. In the meantime, harmonize IV as a six-three, and pass the third up through the fourth (leading note) to the tonic. III, once more, is the first inversion of I ([g]). This is quite an effective fake.

Examples to illustrate the above:

Specimens:

Add two parts above:

Add two parts below:

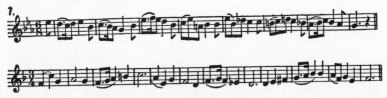

Figuring. Modulation, as such, does not involve anything fresh in the way of figuring, but of course one must remember to prefix the necessary accidentals or corrections to any figures that require them. The specimens above have been figured to serve as an illustration of this, as well as the other points that have been discussed.

This is about the right moment at which to begin the study of counterpoint.

A. THE INVERSIONS OF THE DOMINANT SEVENTH
B. MORE EXTENDED MODULATION

A

The Inversions of the Dominant Seventh

T‌HE inversions of the dominant seventh, in full, are as follows:

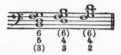

In three parts, the fifth of the original chord, generally speaking, has once more to be omitted, as the root, third and seventh are all essential. That leaves us for the time being with the first and third of the above inversions, as follows:

But the second inversion can be faked with the help of subsidiaries, which may likewise supply the note missing from the other inversions:

In the first inversion (taking once more the dominant seventh of C as our example), the B is the leading note, and resolves upward on to C, while the F (the seventh of the original chord) resolves down to E. In the third inversion, the resolutions are precisely the same, the result being that instead of a diminished fifth (B—F) resolving inwards, we get an augmented fourth (F—B) resolving outwards. In either case, it will be observed, the third note of the chord (the root of the original) can either stay where it is or move to another suitable note of the new chord:

In the second inversion, the F is no longer dissonant with the bass, and its resolution to E is therefore not compulsory, for the interval F—B (or B—F) is now between the upper voices, and accordingly (see p. 5) need not in practice be treated as a dissonance. The resolution to E, however, though no longer obligatory, is still perfectly correct:

What these chords give us, in effect, is of course a set of variants of the perfect and 'interrupted' cadences in their inverted forms. Before going further the student should familiarize himself with the actual handling of the chords by writing a number of such semi-cadences in various major and minor keys, with a few suitable chords leading up to them, so that the whole makes a short musical phrase, or at any rate an intelligible part of one, in this kind of way:

Figuring. The full figurings of these three inversions are respectively $\frac{6}{5}\frac{6}{4}$ and $\frac{6}{4}$. But in practice, even in four parts, these are commonly abbreviated to $\frac{6}{5}\frac{4}{3}$ and $\frac{4}{2}$, and these are the figurings by which they will henceforward be designated. They should be carefully memorized, for these chords are habitually referred to under these designations, and it is a severe handicap to progress if any student has to stop and think what one means when one speaks, for instance, of a 'six-five on B sharp', or a 'four-two on A flat'. He should know instantaneously, just as he knows the meaning of any other common musical term.

These inversions are most useful for the purpose of modulation. It was shown in the last chapter that modulation need not and should not necessarily be effected by means of a full close. Too many full closes in music have an amateurish effect; it is as though one should write English exclusively in short sentences with a full stop at the end of each, ignoring intermediate forms of punctuation and making no use of qualifying or relative clauses, or other niceties of verbal construction. Judicious use of the inversions of the dominant seventh will make it easy to avoid this fault of style. The following exercises (in which modulation is still confined to the 'related' keys) have been specially designed to afford practice in this use, and the student should not go on to the second part of this chapter until he has worked them, after perusal of the specimen workings. Notes marked + are to be harmonized as dominant inversions in the appropriate keys.

Specimens:

Add two parts above:

1.

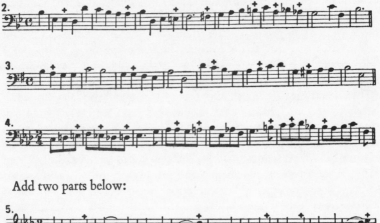

Add two parts below:

B

More Extended Modulation

It is not intended here that anything in the way of remote or abstruse chromatic and enharmonic modulation should be attempted; that is the province of the second volume of this book. But there seems no reason why one should not enlarge, to a certain extent, the restricted field of modulation covered by the five 'related' keys.

The most obvious way to do this is to take advantage of what one may call the 'ambiguity' of the dominant seventh, i.e. the fact that it may resolve either on to the major or the minor of its tonic. Let us take yet once more the familiar key of C major. We have already seen that from this starting point it is the simplest thing in the world to reach the dominants and thence the tonics of A minor, G major, E minor, F major and D minor. The ambiguity of the dominant makes it equally easy, if we are so minded, to land ourselves in A major, G minor, E major, F minor and D major.

And similarly, starting from A minor, we can reach without difficulty the keys of C minor, E major, G minor, D major and F minor.

Clearly our resources have been augmented, at a stroke, to the extent of no less than one hundred per cent. But a word of caution is needed at this point. The keys from which we started contain in themselves no sharps or flats, consequently the keys so far reached from them are all what might be called sweetly reasonable keys—i.e. not one of them contains more than four sharps or flats.

Let us now make the same experiment with two of these 'reasonable' keys, E major and F minor. If from E major we go to G sharp major instead of G sharp minor, we are in a key whose signature would require no lesss than eight sharps—six single and one double. Similarly, if we start from F minor and go to A flat minor instead of A flat major, we have at once a seven-flat key, and further modulation from this point might easily lead us out of our depth, with no enharmonic lifebelt to clutch.

This warning need cause no perturbation of mind. The student will not be required yet awhile to organize his own excursions into these extraneous keys. In the exercises at the end of the chapter this is all done for him, and he will find that keys which would involve the use of more than five sharps or flats in the signature have been avoided altogether, and only at rare intervals will he have a double sharp or flat to negotiate. Moreover, to make his task easier, where a passage contains a modulation to any extraneous key, that key is indicated for him. The 'related' modulations, on the other hand, he will still have to discover and manage for himself.

It is one thing to get into an extraneous key; it is quite another to get out of it and back to the tonic again in an easy and convincing way. It is not enough to scramble home somehow; the return must so be managed that the tonic, when finally reached, must really be felt as the home key and not merely as one more of a series of random modulations. One is continually being surprised to find how easily beginners can contrive to obliterate the sense of the tonic completely, even within the limits of an eight-bar sentence. Two hints for avoiding this particular snag will be found worth remembering:

(1) If your early modulations have been on the 'sharp' side, make a point of touching at least one of the 'flat' keys—i.e. keys with more flats or fewer sharps in the signature than the tonic—before making the final cadence. And vice versa.

(2) If you modulate to an extraneous key and find it difficult from there to reach any of the 'related' keys direct, see if one of their relatives is not accessible. E.g. suppose your principal key is E minor and you have landed yourself (intentionally, we will hope) in G minor. From G minor it is not so easy, without using chromatic or enharmonic means, to reach any of the relatives of E minor *direct*. But it is child's play to go to D minor (dominant of G minor) and thence home via C major, which is a relative of both D minor and E minor.

It only remains to give one or two examples of this kind of procedure:

Add two parts above:

Add two parts below:

Chapter Nine

A. TIED AND DOTTED NOTES
B. SUSPENSIONS (SINGLE)

A. Tied and Dotted Notes

Any essential note may be tied to another note of not greater time-value than itself.

Why the capitals? Because beginners in this field usually produce a lot of chaotic and disjointed work through ignorance or neglect of these two limiting conditions, and they will save themselves and their instructor much waste of time and trouble if they observe them carefully right from the start. If you try to prolong what should be a passing or auxiliary note by tying it over to the succeeding note, you distort the harmony; if you form the habit of (e.g.) tying quavers to minims, you distort the rhythm. Make it an absolute rule, therefore, at any rate until much more experience has been gained, not to do either.

There are two ways of indicating a tie—by a slur, or by a dot. A word or two first of all about the dot.

In simple time, the dot that follows a note means, in effect, that that note is tied to another note of half its own value. In the following, for example, (a) is exactly the same in effect as (b), and (c) as (d):

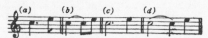

Therefore all that is shortly going to be said about tied notes may be taken as applying equally to dotted notes of this type. The dot, in simple time, is merely one form of the tie.

In compound time, the case is rather different, for the beat-note itself subdivides into three smaller notes and therefore is already dotted. It may still be tied to another note of half its own value; a dotted crotchet, for example, in $\frac{3}{8}$ or $\frac{6}{8}$ time may be tied to a dotted quaver. But such a tie has to be indicated by a slur, not by another dot:

And more often, in compound time, the tie is to a note of one-third or two-thirds the value of the principal note, for which purpose also a slur has to be employed:

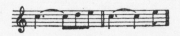

It is only in simple time, therefore, that the student need look suspiciously at the dot, and say to it, 'You are really a tied note.' In compound time—at any rate as far as the full beat-notes are concerned—there is sure to be a slur to catch his eye and warn him what is happening.

There is another case that calls for a word of warning. A note (dotted or otherwise) may be (and often is) tied to another note of its own value. And such a tie is frequently not indicated by a slur, but by substituting a note of double the value:

Here, once more, it will be seen that (a) and (c) are the precise equivalents of (b) and (d) respectively. In (a) and (b), however, the principal note comes on a strong beat, in (c) and (d) on a weak beat.

In the former case either one harmony or two may be used; the following are all perfectly correct:

In the other case two harmonies should (at present) invariably be used. Of the two following, the syncopated harmony of (b) would be irreproachable in composition where this particular effect was desired; one can think of hundreds of such cases (and not only in Schumann). But syncopation lies outside the scope of these elementary exercises, and such an effect, therefore, would be out of place:

So much for the proceedings up to the appearance of the tied note. We must now consider what happens to it after that point.

If the tied note forms a concord with the accompanying parts, it is free, within reason, to move where it likes, up or down, by leap or by step, provided the fundamental decencies of melodic progression are respected.

Subject to this proviso the next note may be short or long, a note of a new chord or a subsidiary of the old one. All the following, for example, are in order:

But the other parts may in the meantime have moved on to another chord of which the tied note does not form a part. In that case it is known as a 'suspension', and is no longer free to go where it will. And that brings us to the second section of this chapter.

B. Suspensions (Single)

When the tied note finds itself in dissonance with the other voices, it has got to 'resolve', i.e. move by step to a concordant note, the other voices meantime remaining where they are until it has done so. (Under certain circumstances they too may move; but for the moment let us confine ourselves to the simplest form of resolution, which is that above described.)

The following points are to be stressed:

(1) The suspended note must come in a stronger accentual position than its note of resolution.

(2) The resolution is usually downwards.

(3) It may, however, be upwards if the step is one of a semitone only.

(4) The suspended note will in most cases be a substantial one—a full beat or a secondary beat.[1] The note of resolution, however, may be a short note, followed by other short notes to complete the beat.

(5) If the suspension is in one of the upper voices, the note of resolution should not be sounded in anticipation by the other, although it may form the bass of the suspension.

A few examples are appended to show how all this works out in practice. P. stands for preparation, S. for suspension, R. for resolution. Look particularly at S. in Ex. 4; this is the augmented triad formed on III of the minor scale. Though diatonic in this context, its markedly dissonant character makes it unsuitable for the beginner to use, except with these safeguards. Its further elucidation is reserved for the second volume.

---

[1] In a moderate 2/4 time, for example, the second and fourth quavers may be regarded as 'secondary' beats. Similarly in 6/8 time, unless the *tempo* is quite a lively one, the third and sixth quavers may be so regarded, at any rate for this purpose.

Examples:

Before going further, the student should write a few similar specimens of his own in various keys and times, and with the suspended note placed by turn in each of the voices, so that he becomes thoroughly familiar with the essential features of the process in its simplest form.

Caution, Consecutive octaves separated only by a suspension are no more to be countenanced than such octaves without the suspension would be. Consecutive fifths similarly separated, however, were tolerated on occasion by most of the great composers. It is only fair to the reader, however, who may have to undergo an examination in this subject, to warn him that this tolerance is unlikely to be shared by his examiners, for examiners seldom take the trouble to find out whether their academic bans and prejudices have any real sanction in classical usage. For example:

Just a word, now, about the exercises which follow. They are in three groups. In the first group (all melodies) the ties and suspensions are introduced or implied in the given part; they need not (and probably cannot) be introduced into the added parts. But merely to harmonize a suspension correctly when you see it is only half the battle, and the smaller half at that. It is of even greater importance to be able to introduce them yourself and treat them correctly, where opportunity offers. And this is just where many students fail conspicuously. In the second and third groups, accordingly, only plain notes have been used in the given parts; the ties and

61

SUSPENSIONS (SINGLE)

suspensions are to be introduced into the added parts. To facilitate this, it must be remembered, it will often be necessary to introduce subsidiary harmony notes on secondary accents and use them as the notes of preparation.

Specimens:

Add two parts below:

Add two parts above, introducing your own suspensions:

SUSPENSIONS (SINGLE)

Add two parts below, again introducing your own suspensions:

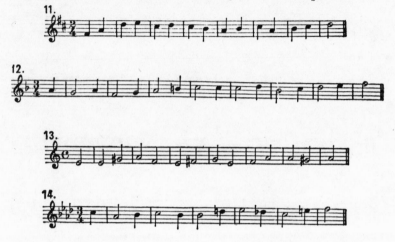

Figuring. When the suspension is in an upper voice, two figures in horizontal alignment are used, the first of them to show the position of the suspended note relative to the bass, the other that of its note of resolution—e.g. 76, 43, etc.

When the suspension is in the bass, figures in vertical alignment show the position of the upper notes from the suspension in the bass, and the horizontal lines which follow show that these notes remain unchanged while the bass resolves.

The figuring of the specimens in the text should make the foregoing explanation enough for the immediate purpose.

Chapter Ten

A. SUSPENSIONS (CONTINUED)
B. DELAYED AND ORNAMENTAL RESOLUTIONS
C. DOUBLE SUSPENSIONS

A. Suspensions (continued)

It has hitherto been assumed that when one note of a chord is suspended, the other voices will remain stationary until its resolution is complete. It is by no means necessary, however, that they should do so.

The general method of combining suspension with movement is best approached by way of counterpoint, of which art it forms a highly important feature. It will therefore not be set forth here. Nor are we concerned, for the moment, with the resolution of a suspended essential seventh on to a new bass note; that is left over until chapter xi.

But there are other procedures; for example, it is always lawful for one of the upper voices to move to another note of the same chord at the instant of resolution:

There are also the progressions indicated respectively by the figurings $\frac{56}{43}$, $\frac{76}{56}$, $\frac{76}{53}$, 96, and 93. In the first three of these, the movement occurs in the upper voice; in the other two cases, it is the bass that moves. Like so many idioms in harmony and counterpoint, these are much more easily grasped from examples than from verbal description, and the following illustrations, with the relevant figurings, should suffice to make clear these essentially simple procedures:

DELAYED AND ORNAMENTAL RESOLUTIONS

It seems unnecessary to write special exercises to give the reader practice in the use of these idioms. He should construct his own examples, similar to those given above, in various keys; he will grasp them much more thoroughly by thus learning to lead up to and introduce them himself than by merely completing them in places indicated beforehand. Students who, at this stage, are unable to perform these very short and simple feats of construction for themselves are unlikely to make any appreciable progress in the practice of harmony; their study of the subject had better be limited to the analysis and classification of chords, and the endeavour to distinguish which notes are essential and which are merely decorative. Even that limited accomplishment is preferable to complete ignorance of harmonic theory.

B. Delayed and Ornamental Resolutions

This again is largely a matter for contrapuntal study. But these ornamental resolutions are so common a feature of every type of music, that it seems desirable to explain them briefly here. Harmony and counterpoint, after all, are so closely related and interdependent that they cannot hope to avoid occasional encroachments on each other's territory.

These ornaments, once more, can be more simply exemplified than described. Here are some of the commonest:

In each case, the true note of resolution is marked with a cross; the note or notes which precede it should be regarded as purely ornamental, even when the first of them happens to be identical with the note of resolution. This, by the way, is of common occurrence, alike in the melody and the bass, and students simply must learn that this and this only is the right way to treat such fragments as the following in any exercise that may be set them:

If they cannot get this into their heads once and for all, they will inevitably fall foul of any examiners they may have to encounter, and they will only have themselves to thank for it.

It will be noticed that the other examples are, in the main, of two types:

(1) Those in which the suspension dips a third before coming back a step to its resolution. If this third is naturally major it is usually best to reduce it to a minor third by raising the lower note chromatically. If the third is already minor, it may (but need not) be reduced to a diminished third, again by raising the lower note chromatically.

If the note of resolution is the semitone *above* the suspension, the ornamental note will, of course, be the note immediately above this, not the note below it.

(2) Those in which the suspension dips (or, much more rarely, rises) to another note of the new chord before proceeding to its note of resolution in that chord. The ornamental note, in such a case, must be that note of the chord which lies nearest to the note of resolution. And the intervening note or notes between them may then also form part of the ornament, if so desired:

One thing more requires explanation, for which this moment seems as good as any other. Very often, the 'suspended' note, instead of being actually suspended, is sung or played again, so that there is no slur or tie to indicate that a process of 'suspension' is taking place. But, once again, the student must learn to recognize this situation at a glance, and to treat the repeated note in every way exactly as if it were suspended. He may with advantage formulate the rule for himself somewhat as follows:

DELAYED AND ORNAMENTAL RESOLUTIONS

In any given bass or melody, when a note is repeated weak to strong, and followed by the note immediately below it, that note can, and very often should, be treated as if it were a suspension.

And in such cases, too, there may be one or more ornamental notes intervening between the 'suspension' and its 'resolution'. The following examples will show what is meant:

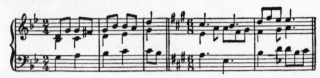

In the exercises which follow, all the notes which are actually suspended are intended to be resolved ornamentally. When the 'suspended' note is, in fact, a repeated note (as described above), the resolutions may be either plain or ornamental, according to context.

Harmonize the following fragments, treating every note as a suspension that can be so treated:

C. Double Suspensions

It is quite possible, in fact it is very common, for two (or, in four-part writing, even three) of the voices to be suspended simultaneously. The suspension is thus not of a single note, but of an interval. The following points are to be noted:

(1) In general, double suspensions of the third or sixth are the commonest and the most satisfactory:

(2) In certain cadential places, however, the leading note and the fourth are often suspended together over a tonic bass, thus forming a double suspension of the augmented fourth or diminished fifth:

(3) Other double suspensions—those of the perfect fourth and fifth, for example—are hazardous in the extreme, except for the highly experienced. That of the octave is forbidden absolutely.

(4) When the suspension is one of the third or sixth, it is common for both voices to resolve in parallels, upwards or downwards, as the case may be (a). But equally, if one of them would naturally resolve downwards and the other upwards, it is quite in order (and may even be necessary) for them to do so (b). In the case of the augmented fourth and diminished fifth, the resolution is always by contrary movement, inwards or outwards as the case may be (c):

DOUBLE SUSPENSIONS

(5) Both resolutions may be plain, or both ornamental; but in the latter event, the form of ornament used had better be the same in both voices (a). If two different forms of ornamentation are used simultaneously, great care must be taken that they form correct and euphonious two-part harmony with one another [(b) and (c)]:

The combination of a plain resolution in one voice with an ornamental one in the other is also quite satisfactory in its effect:

Once more, it will be much the best plan for the student, instead of working set exercises in which he is told exactly what to do and where to do it, to write short phrases and chord-groups for himself, introducing one or more double suspensions (not only in the two upper voices) into each. Let him remember especially (1) that in a true double suspension both suspended notes are dissonant and both accordingly must be prepared; (2) that a full close in any key affords an admirable opportunity for suspensions of this kind.

Figuring. So far as Section A is concerned, the figuring has already been sufficiently explained in the text. As regards Section B, no change in the method of figuring is involved; the suspension and its resolution are indicated in the usual way, while the intervening ornamental notes are ignored. Double suspensions (Section C) are indicated above the bass in just the same manner as single ones according to the position of the suspended notes in relation to the bass—e.g. $\frac{98}{43}$, $\frac{98}{76}$, etc.

When the bass itself is one of the suspended notes, it is not possible to employ the notation used for single bass suspensions. One has to employ two sets of figures, the first of which shows the position of the upper parts from the suspended bass, the second their position from its resolution. The relevant examples in the text have been figured to illustrate this.

Chapter Eleven

SECONDARY DIATONIC CHORDS OF THE
SEVENTH (Root Position)

A. MAJOR KEYS

B. MINOR KEYS

A. Major Keys

THE secondary chords of the seventh, formed on the successive degrees of the scale, are analogous in structure and formation to the chord of the dominant seventh. That is to say, they are formed by adding the seventh note from the bass to the pre-existing triad:

To save circumlocution, they will be referred to henceforth as I_7, II_7, III_7, etc.

One note, of course, has to be omitted in three-part work, and as a rule (just as in the case of the dominant seventh) the fifth is the note that can safely be left out. But if the fifth is a diminished and not a true fifth, as in II_7 minor and VII_7 both major and minor, then the fifth may equally well be left in and the third omitted:

Two other points have to be considered, the treatment of the seventh itself, and the treatment of the bass.

Regarding the seventh itself, keep these points in mind:

(1) The seventh should be prepared, i.e. it should appear as an essential note in the chord immediately preceding. To this extent it is a 'suspended' note, and this is what was meant when we spoke on p. 65 of 'a suspended essential seventh'. Unlike other suspensions, however, it need not necessarily be given a stronger accentual position than the note on which it resolves. Its effect is more telling, none the less, when it *is* given a strong accent.

This habit of treating the secondary sevenths as *prepared* discords was pretty generally observed by all composers from the seventeenth century till the later part of the nineteenth. In the work of J. S. Bach, for example, the observances vastly outnumber the exceptions, and beginners will certainly be well advised to follow his example in this respect.

(2) The resolution of the seventh, like that of the dominant seventh, is normally downwards and by step. But if it happens to be a major seventh, as in the case of I$_7$ and IV$_7$ in the major keys, then it may equally well resolve upwards by semitone, while the bass (to anticipate) moves down a third:

The bass, apart from the special case just considered, will follow the example, once more, of the dominant seventh and either rise a fourth (or fall a fifth, which comes to the same thing) or rise one step. But these alternatives are not equally good for all the sevenths. In particular:

I$_7$. This should resolve on IV rather than on II.

II$_7$ and III$_7$. These likewise are not well suited by a stepwise resolution. They should resolve on V and VI respectively rather than on III and IV, being influenced in this matter by the natural affinities and antipathies of the corresponding triads (see ch. ii, p. 14).

II$_7$ may resolve on V$_7$ just as well as on V. And if taken on a weak beat, the resolution may be delayed by the interposition of a 'cadential' six-four on the following strong beat;

IV$_7$. This naturally goes to V and not to VII (except in certain types of four-part sequence: see Part II, ch. xxiv). It may also, in four-part work, resolve comfortably on V$_7$; but with only three parts, this progression calls for a little faking:

VI$_7$. The resolution to II or II$_7$ is good, but equally so, in four parts, is the stepwise resolution to the dominant six-five (a). In three-part work, however, the latter is not so handy. Rather wide spacing is required (b): an alternative resolution is to the diminished triad on the leading note, which in turn must resolve on to I (c):

VII. Either I or III gives an adequate resolution; the former, of course, has a markedly cadential character:

From what has been said above, it will be gathered that these diatonic sevenths lend themselves more readily, in certain respects, to four-part than to three-part use. And this applies as much, or more, to their inversions. Their essential features, none the less, can perfectly well be introduced in three-part writing, and the student who masters them first in this form will find it very much easier to handle them later in four parts than if he has approached them from the first as exclusively four-part chords.

There seems no occasion to set special exercises on the use of these chords within the limits of a single key, whether major or minor. Some will be found at the end of the chapter; these involve simple modulations to related keys and should therefore not be attempted until Section B (minor keys) has also been studied. They are only short exercises in any case, as extended periods involving the constant use of chords of a particular type are apt to sound stilted and artificial.

For the time being, the student should practice himself in the preparation, formation, and resolution of single chords in various major keys and on various degrees of the scale, taking care sometimes to place the seventh in the middle as well as in the upper voice. Then he can go on to write slightly longer phrases, still without modulation, somewhat on the following lines:

B. *Minor Keys*

So many variants of these chords are made possible by the formation of the melodic minor scale that it will be convenient in the first place to tabulate them all for the purposes of reference, using C minor as our norm:

Some of the above (those bracketed) may be eliminated for the present purpose. In three-part writing, be it remembered, we shall continue to leave in the third and omit the fifth when the latter is a perfect fifth; therefore II₇B and III₇A may be left out of account for the time being (something will have to be said about them, however, in ch. xxiv). V₇ is the dominant seventh, already covered in ch. vii. The forms VII₇C and VII₇D, though theoretically diatonic in the key of C minor, are of little or no practical use in that key, as they have no satisfactory resolution. We may begin, therefore, by eliminating these five from our list, and proceed to examine the remainder briefly one by one, remembering always that the general principles already laid down for the preparation and resolution of discordant notes will apply in every case.

I₇ A. Resolve on to IV.

I₇ B. Resolve on to VI (B upwards to C).

II₇ A. Resolve on to V or V₇.

III₇ B. Resolve on to VI or I. If the chord is completed by the augmented fifth from the bass instead of the third, remember that *both* upper parts are dissonant and must consequently be prepared:

IV₇ A. The best three-part resolution is to VII₇ A or VII₇ B. The resolution to V₇ is easy in four parts but has to be faked in three parts:

IV₇ B. In three parts, resolve on to V; in four parts V₇ is also feasible:

V₇ A. I₇A is the best resolution; the chord is seldom useful in C minor.

VI₇ A. Resolve on to IV (G upwards to A♭).

VI₇ B. Resolve on to the dominant six-five, or the diminished triad on the leading note, according to position and spacing, exactly as prescribed for the same chord in a major key. Either the third or the fifth may be omitted from this chord; the resolution will be the same in both cases.

VII₇ A. Not very often required; the resolution is to III or III₇

VII₇ B. This is the only diatonic chord of the diminished seventh. It requires no preparation, though it is often prepared. Either the third or the fifth may be omitted, and alike in three and four parts the leading note in the bass must rise to the tonic, so that the resolution is to I:

Figuring. Exactly as in the case of the dominant seventh except that a cross stroke is usually added to the tail of the 7 if the seventh is diminished:₸

Preliminary exercises should now be carried out on precisely the same lines as suggested above for the major keys, eg.:

In the exercises which follow, the sign + has been used to show that a seventh of some sort is to be used there; but the student will have to discover for himself what kind of a seventh it is, in what key, and whether the 'suspended' note is more conveniently taken by the top or the middle voice. Basses only are provided, as melodies by themselves, where these chords are concerned, usually fail to convey a sufficiently clear and precise indication of the implied harmonic progression.

Add two parts above:

Chapter Twelve

INVERTED FORMS OF THE SECONDARY DIATONIC SEVENTHS

A. FIRST INVERSIONS
B. SECOND INVERSIONS
C. THIRD INVERSIONS

Tʜɪꜱ chapter will not be a long one. It has already been stated that more effective and extensive use can be made of these chords in four-part writing than in three-part, and their fuller treatment is accordingly reserved for Part II. For the time being the object is merely to enable the student to get the general 'feel' of the chords, and some idea of their normal mode of resolution.

A. First Inversions

In these, as in the corresponding inversion of the dominant seventh, the fifth of the original chord (i.e. the third of the chord in its inverted form) has to be omitted, for the third has now become the bass, and the root and the seventh (both indispensable) have to be assigned to the two upper voices.

The dissonant element in the chord, therefore, is the fifth from the bass, and this is the note that has to be prepared and resolved. Note, moreover, that its resolution is invariably downwards, while the bass proceeds upwards by step. The third voice, meantime, can remain unchanged or move to any other convenient note that forms a suitable harmony with the other two:

For the moment, all the student need do by way of exercise is to prac-tise himself in the preparation, formation, and resolution of this chord in various major and minor keys. Of the alternative minor forms listed as admissible in Section B₇ of the last chapter, I₇B, IV₇A and V₇A will be found more or less unsuitable for this inversion in three-part work. It must be remembered, moreover, that if IV₇B or VI₇B is inverted in any position, the raised sixth of the minor scale is still bound to proceed upwards to the leading note.

79

INVERTED FORMS OF DIATONIC SEVENTHS

B. Second Inversions

From most of these chords (speaking in terms of their root positions) it is preferable, as with the dominant seventh, to omit the fifth rather than the third, so that the second inversions, for the most part, are not available for three-part use. But where the fifth of the chord is a *diminished* fifth (VII₇ in the major keys, II₇A and VII₇B in the minor) it may be retained instead of the third with quite good effect, so that second inversions of these three chords are serviceable in three-part writing. The dissonant note now becomes the third from the bass, and when it resolves, the bass likewise moves down a step with it. The normal resolutions of the three chords are then as follows:

Practice them in various keys till you are sure you can cope with them; they are useful for mixing purposes.

C. Third Inversions

The seventh of the original chord now becomes the bass, and this resolves downwards. It will be found that in minor keys the forms I₇B, II₇B, IV₇A, V₇A and VI₇A are all awkward to prepare, or to resolve, or both. Nor is VII₇B of much use, as the resolution is to a six-four chord which must be of the 'passing' type, and is therefore serviceable only in one context:

The remainder, however, are all quite useful. Once more, it will generally be found preferable to give the third of the original chord preference over the fifth, except in the case of VII₇ in the major, II₇A and VII₇B in the minor keys, where the false fifth (the sixth from the bass in this inversion) is at least as good in effect as the third. The bass, being the seventh, resolves downwards, and the other parts normally adjust themselves so as to form a six-three chord on the new bass note:

As before, have a little preliminary practice with these chords before proceeding to the set exercises at the end of the chapter. These exercises, like those appended to the previous chapter, are merely short modulating phrases intended to give practice in all three inversions of the chords. All these inversions, once more, are marked with a cross, but the student will have to discover for himself which inversion and in which key, gives the best result.

Figuring. Exactly the same as in the corresponding inversions of the dominant seventh.

Specimens:

INVERTED FORMS OF DIATONIC SEVENTHS

Add two parts above:

Chapter Thirteen

ADDITIONAL METHODS OF MELODIC[1] DECORATION

A. CHROMATIC UNACCENTED PASSING NOTES
B. ACCENTED PASSING AND AUXILIARY NOTES (DIATONIC)
C. ACCENTED PASSING AND AUXILIARY NOTES (CHROMATIC)

CHAPTER IV dealt with the simplest means of melodic decoration, that is to say, unaccented passing and auxiliary notes and secondary harmony notes. Even these modest resources were found to add greatly to the interest of the work by diversifying its texture. With the help of those now to be made available, a very much longer step can be made in the same direction. It will be found, too, that although these embellishments are in their nature melodic (in the sense defined in the footnote), and add nothing to the basic harmonic material so far acquired, they nevertheless add much to the actual harmonic effect by exploiting the use of accented unessential dissonance. Though they sometimes involve the use of chromatic notes, the result is not to be described as chromatic harmony. That term implies the use of chords containing one or more *essential* notes foreign to the key in which they occur, and this subject is left over for treatment in the first part of the second volume.

A. Chromatic Unaccented Passing Notes

These notes are a commonplace of instrumental composition, where they are employed with the utmost freedom. To voices, however, they are much less congenial, for voices are far less agile than instruments, and moreover have an inherent difficulty in the accurate intonation of extended semitonic passages. For present purposes, they had better be restricted to the two following functions:

(1) As single passing notes in between two essential notes lying a whole tone apart from one another. The passing note is formed by raising chromatically the first of the essential notes:

---

[1] Using this term in its broadest sense—i.e. with reference to the construction of any single part, as opposed to the chordal progressions formed by the parts in combination. It is not intended for a moment to suggest that only the 'melody' (i.e. the top part) is amenable to the decorative processes about to be described.

It may be found by experiment that this device (which should in any case be used very sparingly) is only applicable in major keys. The best notes for the purpose are the fifth notes of I, IV, and V, and the corresponding notes (i.e. the third from the bass) of their first inversions. In four-part writing the fifth note of V_7 and third of VII_7 (and correspondingly of their inversions) may likewise be augmented:

(2) As companions to ordinary passing notes, whether in simple or compound time, when the two essential notes lie a third apart. In this case the second passing note is commonly but not necessarily formed by raising the first one chromatically:

It may well be asked at this point why only the *raising* of notes chromatically should have been mentioned. Cannot they also be lowered?

The answer is, guardedly, 'yes'. Such a cadence as the following, for example, is correct enough and euphonious enough in its own way:

But these downward-passing notes are tricky things to handle. At best they achieve a certain languishing elegance; at worst—and with what fatal ease!—they degenerate into mawkishness or triviality. Only the tact of a Mozart can perceive unerringly when and how to use them. *Verb. sap.*

The same applies to downward-going chromatic accented passing notes and appoggiaturas. Only the upward-moving kind, therefore, will be considered in Sections C of this chapter and A of the next.

B. *Accented Passing and Auxiliary Notes (Diatonic)*

An accented passing note, as its name implies, is a passing note taken on the accent instead of between accents. Its passage is usually downwards, and the note preceding it may be either an essential note of the previous chord or another (unaccented) passing or auxiliary note:

The note on which the dissonance is to resolve may be sounded in anticipation (as in the case of suspension) by the bass (a) but preferably not by an upper voice, whether in three-part or four-part writing (b and c).

The passage may also be upwards (again as in the case of suspensions) if the movement is by semitone:

But also (in the upper voices only) a passing note that is the minor seventh from the bass may rise with good effect to the octave (a), and in all voices the sixth note of the scale may pass up to the leading note if the harmony is V or V_7 in any position (b):

Apart from the above, upward-passing notes in the bass should only be used in a very cautious and circumspect manner. The safest are those leading from the root of a common chord to its first inversion:

Doublings in thirds (tenths) or sixths may be freely used in a downward direction between any two parts (a). Upward-going doublings in thirds or sixths are also feasible between upper voices (b). If the passing note rises in the bass it can likewise be doubled in thirds (tenths), but seldom or never in sixths (c):

In cases (b) and (c) above, observe that one of the notes rising in pairs may be a note which would have preferred to fall had it been single.

Now for accented auxiliary notes. These are precisely similar, so far as their resolution is concerned, to accented passing notes. The same conditions determine whether they rise or fall; if the reader will peruse the subjoined examples, he should need no further verbal elucidation:

Before working the longer exercises at the end of the chapter (which include both diatonic and chromatic notes) the student had better try his hand at the short phrases which follow. He may well supplement these by taking some of the simpler exercises from an earlier chapter—chapter iv, for example, and re-working them suitably. Here are the last of the basses and the first of the melodies from that set re-treated in this manner to show just what is meant:

Add two parts above:

Add two parts below:

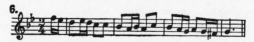

C. Accented Passing and Auxiliary Notes (Chromatic)

[It has already been explained that we are only going to consider, for the time being at any rate, the upward-going variety of these chromatic unessential notes.]

Passing notes of this kind are formed by raising the previous note chromatically. This note may be either an essential note or an unaccented passing note. The resolution is necessarily upwards, and there is no objection to the note of resolution being sounded by anticipation (in any lower voice). Indeed, this tends to enhance the effect of the dissonance, but is not always feasible in three-part writing.

The treatment of accented (lower) auxiliary notes is precisely similar to that of the passing notes. Once more, the preceding note may be either an essential or a passing note. In the latter event, by the way, the term 'auxiliary' is not quite accurate, for an auxiliary note, by definition, is taken between two statements of the same *essential* note. But there is no other term which will serve, so let it pass.

Accented chromatic passing notes are in the main unsuitable for use in the bass, and even in the upper parts are more effective if not used with undue frequency. The auxiliary kind, however, can be employed occasionally in the bass, but the preceding note in this event must be an essential note:

The following short phrases will serve to exemplify the various points mentioned in the preceding paragraphs:

Figuring. No indication is given in the bass when the unessential notes are in the upper voices. Figured bass applies in the main to essential harmonies; unessential embellishments were left, as a matter of historical tradition, to the discretion of the performer.

When there is an accented passing note in the bass, two sets of figures have to be inserted, showing the positions in regard to both the dissonant note and its resolution, exactly as in the case of suspensions. An alternative method is to figure the essential note only, with a sloping dash or other distinguishing mark above the passing note:

This is quite a convenient method; it is, however, a modern expedient and forms no part of the traditional method of figuring.

The following exercises give scope for the use of all the resources explained in this chapter. The student is required not only to recognize the unessential where it figures in the given part but also (more particularly where the bass is given) to introduce it at his discretion into the other parts.

Add two parts above:

89

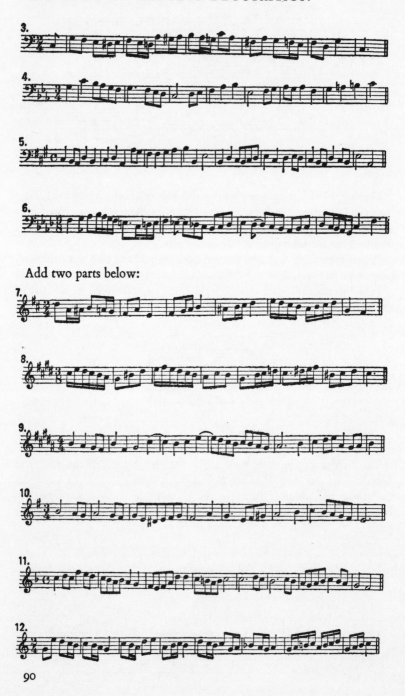

Add two parts below:

Chapter Fourteen

ADDITIONAL METHODS OF MELODIC DECORATION (CONTINUED)

A. APPOGGIATURAS
B. ANTICIPATIONS
C. CHANGING NOTES

A. Appoggiaturas

AN appoggiatura closely resembles an accented passing note. The points of difference are:

(1) It may be (and usually is) approached by leap.

(2) It may be of relatively long value—as long as, or even longer than, the note on which it resolves.

It may be either diatonic or chromatic. In the latter event, as already stated, it will be a chromatically raised note with an upward resolution.

The following examples will show exactly what is meant, the appoggiaturas being marked with a cross:

Short appoggiaturas:

[handwritten: NOT P/NOTE— Because approached by leap—not step.]

Long appoggiaturas:

Appoggiaturas—and for that matter accented passing notes too—may be given an ornamental form of resolution by jumping up or down a third according as the resolution is upwards or downwards. In the latter case the third, if naturally major, should be reduced to a minor third by raising the lower ornamental note chromatically. If the third is naturally minor, it may (but need not) be similarly converted into a diminished third. Once more, a few examples will suffice to make the above quite easy to grasp.

Short appoggiaturas and accented passing notes:

G

Long appoggiaturas:

Note that if the appoggiatura is lower than the essential note (i.e. if it resolves upwards), it is best approached from above; if higher, from below. This applies equally whether the resolution be plain or ornamental.

B. Anticipations

The term explains itself; to save long-winded and possibly unilluminating definition, here are two examples of the simplest type, which cannot but be familiar to everybody who has ever heard any music:

In the above, note two points:

(1) The anticipation is an *unessential* note and as such is approached by step. This is part of the definition of the term, in its strictest sense. We shall soon see, however, that in practice it is of more extended application.

(2) Anticipatory notes may be doubled in thirds or sixths in the upper parts. If single, they are more effective in the melody itself than in the middle voices (though Bach not infrequently uses them in alto or tenor) and should in no case be assigned to the bass.

But the term 'anticipation', as already hinted, has wider application than would appear from the above simple cadential formulae. Consider the following passage, for example:

Here, the second, fourth and sixth notes in each bar of the melody are 'anticipations' in the sense of being identical with the note that is coming next. It is customary and convenient so to describe them, but only the sixth note of the second bar is an anticipation in the strictest sense of the term. The others are either subsidiary harmony notes (in which case, of course, they may be approached by leap) or essential notes preceded by an accented passing note.

It is also quite possible for an anticipation and its following note both to be unessential:

Or the anticipation may itself be the resolution of a previous suspension:

It will thus be seen that in figures of this kind, so many alternative methods of treating each pair of notes are available, that no serious difficulty need arise for any one who keeps a clear head.

For study of this type of figuration in its most sublimated and transcendental form, readers may be referred (if it has not come spontaneously into their minds) to the instrumental accompaniment of the last chorus in Part I of Bach's Passion (St. Matthew).

C. Changing Notes

It is not proposed here to go exhaustively into the matter of 'changing notes', as these are (or should be) fully explained in text-books on counterpoint, and it may therefore be presumed that the reader, by this time, is already familiar with them. But there are certain extensions of this idiom which lie rather outside the boundaries of pure counterpoint, and these may be advantageously considered here.

It will be remembered that these 'changing notes' so far as counterpoint is concerned, are considered in four different patterns:

Of the above, the last is marked with a query, as it is apt to produce a certain awkwardness or bumpiness which disturbs the flow of the contrapuntal pattern, and beginners are therefore discouraged from using it. But for our present purpose it has to be examined as well as the other three.

In counterpoint, all the above patterns are used within the limits of a single harmony, the first and fourth notes alone being regarded as essential. The notes in between (the 'changing notes') are without harmonic significance.

In harmony, however, these same figures can be used on a two-chord basis. Let us consider (a) and (b) together first, then (c) and (d).

In this harmonic adaptation of (a) and (b) it will be found that the first note is still an essential note, the second an unessential. The third note may be an essential note of the next chord, or it may be an accented unessential note, leaving the fourth note to be either a passing or an essential note as the case may be:

Similarly with (c) and (d). The third note may be an essential note, or it may be an accented passing note (or appoggiatura, if you prefer to call it so in this position). In the case of (c) it should then be raised chromatically if necessary to provide the semitonic resolution upwards:

The exercises which follow are of two kinds. The first consist of short melodic phrases, by way of preliminary practice. In these the decoration is already there in the given part, and the student's only real problem is to make up his mind which notes are essential and which unessential, bearing in mind that many of the latter may well be chromatic. Sharps, flats, and naturals, therefore—sharps and naturals more particularly—are to be viewed with a certain amount of suspicion.

It will be apparent from the conformation of the given melodies that some are intended primarily for practice in appoggiaturas, others in anticipations, while others again are diversified in pattern, embodying the work of the chapter as a whole.

Specimens:

Add two parts below:

In the remainder of the exercises, the bass is given, and the student is required to introduce 'decorations according to taste' in the added parts, more particularly in the melody, the bass itself being for the most part very simple, not to say bare, in character. If the beginner finds it difficult at first to 'think decoratively', let him begin by adding an equally simple melody, and then embellish it. Some find this the easier way; here are two examples of the process, the essential outline of the bass being identical in both:

Decoration (I)

Decoration (II)

Add two parts above:

1.

2.

3.

4.

Figuring. As far as anticipations, changing notes, and 'short' appoggiaturas are concerned, no indications need be given in the figuring. 'Long' appoggiaturas, however, can be conveniently indicated; the examples in Section A have been figured accordingly to show the method.

PART II

Chapter Fifteen

PRELIMINARY REMARKS ON FOUR-PART WRITING

PART II is planned in the main as a recapitulation, chapter by chapter, of Part I, the only difference being that we are now and henceforward concerned with harmony in four parts, and not (as hitherto) in three. This recapitulation extends up to the end of chapter xxvii; the last two chapters break new ground, being concerned respectively with chords of the ninth (necessarily omitted from Part I, as they cannot be used in fewer than four parts) and with the harmonization of chorales. Any real understanding of Bach's polyphony presupposes an acquaintance with his work in this field, where his harmonic principles and methods are revealed in their simplest and most quintessential form. This final chapter, it is hoped, will enable the reader to lay the foundation of such an understanding.

From a purely harmonic point of view, four-part writing has obvious advantages over three-part. The chords are richer and fuller, and offer greater variety in the way of spacing and distribution. In the matter of texture, however, the advantage is far from being all on one side. Three-part writing enjoys delightful freedom of manœuvre; the voices are by no means disposed to get in one another's way, and it is thus easy to make all of them reasonably interesting, and so rid oneself once and for all of the mistaken idea that the claims of harmony are necessarily at variance with those of counterpoint. In four-part work this reconcilation is more difficult. The middle parts have less elbow-room, and there is increased danger of writing consecutive fifths and octaves or other awkward progressions.

The beginner in four parts may therefore feel somewhat cramped at the outset. The advice usually given him is to move the parts as little as possible and to allow any of them to go on repeating the same note as long as the harmonic progression makes it feasible to do so. 'Safety First', in fact, is the maxim enjoined.

This advice is sound enough as far as it goes. But if followed blindly and consistently, it results in a painful costiveness of the inner parts. It is all very well for alto or tenor to have an occasional bar like this:

99

But it is not at all well for either of them to have three or four such bars in succession, like this:

Inertia of this kind can often be overcome, if no other remedy can be found, by crossing the two middle parts. Let it be remembered that the upper octave of the tenor coincides, roughly speaking, with the lower octave of the alto. Within this range it is perfectly permissible for alto and tenor to cross for a beat or two, and the student need have no hesitation in making them do so whenever considerations of musical texture make it expedient. Consider, for example, the following:

The lurking menace of possible consecutives is exposed in the first example. The second shows how, by a momentary cross between alto and tenor, the danger can very easily be avoided.

One may add, too, that an *occasional* unorthodoxy or even eccentricity of spacing or doubling is readily condoned for the sake of good part-writing and attractiveness of texture. Note, however, that the word 'occasional' is printed in italics.

Now for a few words about the exercises to be worked. No new exercises are provided in Part II except in chapters xxv, xxviii, and xxix. Apart from these, the exercises set in Part I are to do duty again, but they must be re-worked, of course, in four parts instead of three. For this purpose many of them will have to be transposed. The vocal layout, so far as Part II is concerned, will invariably be S.A.T.B. Where the given part is already a soprano or bass, of course, no transposition will be needed. But if it is an alto, with other parts to be added below, it must be transposed up so that it becomes a soprano. And similarly, if it is a tenor, with other parts to be added above, it must be transposed down, so that it becomes a bass. And even in the exercises where no transposition is required, it will often be found that a completely new working is necessary. It might be possible, every now and again, to take the original three-part working as it stands and merely add a fourth part of appropriate compass. It might also be feasible in some cases to retain the two outer parts of the original working and add fresh parts for A. and T., provided that the outer parts are sufficiently far apart from one another to admit of two parts being fitted in between them. But for the most part an entirely new version is likely to give the best result.

Great care must still be taken with the layout. Even with four parts, the maximum distance between the two outer voices should never exceed two octaves and a fifth at any given point, and the great majority of the chords should lie well within this limit. Undue extension of the vocal framework is one of the commonest faults of beginners' work; it requires prompt and ruthless correction from the instructor.

COMMON CHORDS IN ROOT POSITION
(MAJOR KEYS ONLY)

A. Spacing

THE general principles of spacing still hold good; that is to say, wide gaps between any two voices should be avoided as far as is reasonably possible, except between tenor and bass. In that region gaps up to an octave and a third are by no means infrequent, especially when the upper voices are closely spaced. Even an octave and a fifth may occasionally be found under those conditions, but this must be regarded as the extreme limit:

B. Doubling and Omission of Notes

In four-part writing, one note of a triad has necessarily to be doubled. Other things being equal, the root is the best note to double. But other things are frequently not equal, and then the fifth or third may be doubled without hesitation, always provided that the latter does not happen to be the leading note of the key.

Even in four-part writing, it will often be found convenient to omit the fifth of the chord. In that case, the root is usually present in triplicate, with a single third somewhere to complete the chord. But occasionally the natural leading of the voices will make it expedient to double both root and third:

The effect of this is quite satisfactory, but the situation can hardly arise as long as common chords only are employed, unless passing notes are also present (as in the above example).

C. Mutual Relationship of Chords in Progression

This is not affected in any way by the introduction of a fourth voice. There is, however, a greatly increased risk of writing prohibited consecutives, especially between alto and bass on the one hand or soprano and tenor on the other. The beginner is hereby warned, accordingly, to keep an extra sharp look-out in those quarters.

Specimens from Chapter II, reworked in four parts:

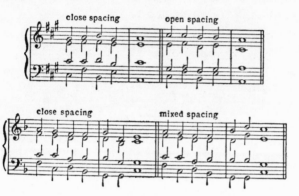

COMMON CHORDS IN ROOT POSITION
(MINOR KEYS)

IT may be as well to remind the student that the sharpened sixth of the melodic minor—F sharp, for example, in A minor—is bound to rise to the leading note, and therefore must not be doubled, on account of the consecutive octaves which would result. Therefore in IIA, double the root or third; in IVA, the root or fifth:

In the progression VA to VI (the 'interrupted' cadence) it will be found by experiment that the third note of VI, although a major third, has got to be doubled, as any other doubling involves faulty progression of one sort or another:

Very few beginners seem able to retain this simple maxim in their heads, even when the necessity has been fully explained to them. Those who do are able in this way to save themselves a great deal of merited objurgation from their instructor.

Specimens from Chapter III re-worked in four parts:

FIRST INVERSIONS OF THE COMMON CHORD

WHEN using the first inversion of VII, remember that the sixth note of this chord is the leading note, and therefore the bass or third should be doubled in preference to it. This restriction does not apply, be it observed, to the first inversion of II in the minor key, which is equally a diminished triad, but does not contain the leading note.

Chords of the sixth formed on successive degrees of the scale offer an insidious opportunity for writing consecutive fifths, or octaves, or both. The best safeguard against this is to move the two outer parts in parallel sixths, and to see at the same time that neither of the other parts doubles a similar note in two successive chords. That is to say, if in the first chord the sixth is doubled, let the bass or third be doubled in the next, and so on:

It has already been made clear that the doubling of the major third of a triad, or the corresponding note of its inversion (the bass) is not the crime it is commonly supposed to be. The bass of such an inversion (always provided it is not the leading note) can in fact be doubled with admirable effect either by soprano or tenor:

Doubling by the alto is more questionable in effect; but Bach permits himself such doubling whenever the natural leading of the voices makes it convenient. Very many examiners, however, seem to be quite unaware of the countless precedents which he has set for this usage.

There is one special use of the first inversion of III, both in major and minor keys, which calls for a word of explanation here, as it seemed premature to enter into such details in the fourth chapter of Part I. When a melody moves from the mediant to the tonic in what appears to be a cadential or quasi-cadential progression, the mediant should be harmonized with a first inversion of III, which is regarded, in such cases, as the functional equivalent of a dominant chord, and is, in fact, the simplest form of what some theorists classify as a 'dominant thirteenth':

In the above usage note carefully that:

(1) The sixth of the chord (the 'thirteenth' so-called) invariably appears as a melody note—i.e. in the top part.

(2) Its progression is invariably down to the tonic, so that it cannot be doubled. Nor can the third, which is the leading note, so that the bass (the dominant) is perforce doubled either by alto or tenor.

(3) In the minor key, the chord thus inverted will be IIIA, not III, which has no cadential force.

[It may conveniently be added here (to save devoting a special chapter to it in future) that either of these dominant notes may be replaced by a dominant seventh, which then resolves downwards by step in the usual way:

This gives us the true 'dominant thirteenth' in two of its three possible positions. In the remaining one, the leading note is in the bass, and the resolution is exactly as one would expect:

The chord is, in truth, of very minor importance and not worth a quarter of the attention some theorists have bestowed upon it. It is not proposed to set any exercises in the use of it, or to honour it undeservedly by any further reference in this volume.]

FIRST INVERSIONS OF COMMON CHORD

Specimens from Chapter IV, re-worked in four parts:

UNACCENTED PASSING AND AUXILIARY NOTES (DIATONIC): SUBSIDIARY HARMONY NOTES

So far as theory goes, the introduction of the fourth part makes no difference whatever; the text of Chapter V may be taken just as it stands, without amplification.

In practice, just one caution is necessary. Beginners are apt to crowd the work and get themselves into unnecessary difficulties by trying to double or re-double too many unessential or subsidiary notes at once. In doing so they sometimes forget what is by very definition the characteristic of a passing or auxiliary note, viz. that it is *both approached and quitted by step*. Consider the following:

In the above (a) and (b) both typify this kind of error, and both are of regrettably common occurrence. In (a), the basic harmony of the second beat is the first inversion of the D minor chord. The C in the tenor, being approached by leap, destroys this harmony, and produces the awkward effect of a change of chord (C major) on the passing note E in the bass. In (b) the harmony of the second beat is A minor, and once more the tenor spoils the effect by putting in a D which does not pass but remains in anticipation of the D major chord which is to follow. Like the C in the first example, it is badly misplaced, and both notes should be omitted, as shown in (d) and (e) above.

Specimens from Chapter V (Section C) re-worked in four parts:

Chapter Twenty
(Recapitulation of *Chapter Six*)

THE SIX-FOUR CHORD

Two points only come up here for special consideration, viz. doubling, and the use of the 'passing' six-four chord.

As regards doubling, one can but repeat the caution already given that the fourth from the bass, being a quasi-dissonance, ought not to be doubled as a principal note. The occasional doubling of it as a subsidiary · note, as already explained (p. 39), is a recognized licence which may be taken just as well in four parts as in three.

The best note to double is undoubtedly the bass, but the sixth is quite a tolerable alternative in case of need.

Now we have to consider the case of the 'passing' six-four. The chord is generally limited to two positions—the supertonic (second inversion of V) and the dominant (second inversion of I). Here are examples to show the manner in which it is used:

It will be apparent from the above that the chord has to be kept in a strait-waistcoat. Note the following specific points:

(1) The bass of the chord is doubled by the top voice (this is not absolutely essential but it is undoubtedly the best layout for this purpose).

(2) In both outer parts this note is both approached and quitted by step in contrary movement. The chord thus serves as a kind of bridge between I and its first inversion, or between IV and its first inversion.

(3) It may take either a weak or a strong accent. The present author greatly prefers the latter, but this view is not shared by other writers on this subject.

It should be added that these two forms of the 'passing' six-four are by no means of equal utility. When the progression is from I to its first inversion, the intervening chord need not be a six-four at all. The six-three on the same note (first inversion of VII) is always available as an alternative, and is always to be preferred:

When the progression is from IV to its first inversion (or vice versa), this alternative is not available. The intervening chord is still under no compulsion to be a six-four; the dominant triad and dominant seventh can both be used in this position. But the passing six-four is often a convenient alternative. It is never more than that, and hence has no claim to more than a lowly rank in the hierarchy of chords.

There is, however, one other use of it still to be exemplified;

The six-four here, it will be noticed, is still the second inversion of I. But the outer parts are no longer moving in contrary motion, but in parallel sixths, so that the upper note of the six-four is no longer the doubled bass note, but the sixth. This is really the most satisfactory of all the passing six-fours, and Bach often avails himself of it as an approach to a cadence when the conformation of the melody makes it possible.

This variant (unlike the other two) is quite usable in three-part work; but it seemed better to defer consideration of it until this chapter, instead of treating it as an isolated case in Chapter VI.

It should be added that all the above remarks about the passing six-four are equally applicable whether the key is major or minor. The examples given are all in C major. Put three flats in the signature, sharpen the leading note where necessary, and they will serve their purpose just as well in the new key.

No special exercises in this use of the chord need be set; but some or all of the exercises in Chapter VI should be re-worked, as usual, in four parts. Specimen:

Chapter Twenty-One
(Recapitulation of *Chapter Seven*)

A. THE CHORD OF THE DOMINANT SEVENTH
(ROOT POSITION)
B. MODULATION (FIRST STAGE)

A. *The Chord of the Dominant Seventh*

THE addition of a fourth part obviates the necessity for leaving out one note of this four-note chord. The fifth remains to some extent, however, a redundant note, and may still be omitted at discretion. In this case, naturally, it is the root that has to be doubled, as the other notes of the chord (the seventh and the leading note) do not admit of duplication. In the following four-part cadences, for example, the alternative forms (a) and (b) are equally acceptable:

It will be noticed above that the fifth has got to be omitted from one of the two chords forming the cadence, and it really does not matter which.

Specimens from Chapter VII, re-worked in four parts:

B. *Modulation (The First Stage)*

Modulation, as such, does not involve the use of any chord other than those already considered, and is therefore unaffected, in principle, by the addition of the fourth part. In practice, this addition will be found to make modulation rather easier than it was before.

MODULATION

Further speciments from Chapter VII, re-worked in four parts:

Chapter Twenty-Two
(Recapitulation of *Chapter Eight*)

A. THE INVERSIONS OF THE DOMINANT SEVENTH
B. MORE EXTENDED MODULATION

A. *The Inversions of the Dominant Seventh*

LET us consider first of all the first and third inversions, as these two in the main, formed the subject matter of Chapter VIII.

These, of course, may now be complete; but it is still perfectly feasible to omit the fifth of the original chord and to double its root. The following progressions, for example, are all quite sound, though the omission of the fifth is perhaps more noticeable, especially in the case of the six-five, than when the chord is in root position:

It remains to amplify what has already been said (Chapter VIII), about the four-three. From this, the second inversion, no note can be omitted, as the only redundant note of the original chord (the fifth) now forms the bass of the inversion, so that there is no question of leaving it out. The seventh of the original chord (as already observed) is no longer dissonant with the bass, and is therefore under no compulsion to resolve downwards, though of course it is still at perfect liberty to do so:

This chord is undoubtedly the weakest of the three inversions, and beginners frequently use it in places where a plain six-three chord would be much more effective. Both Bach and Handel seem to have viewed the chord with marked distaste, if one can judge by the rarity of its employment in their compositions. In Bach's chorales, its appearances could almost be numbered on one's fingers, and he practically confines himself to one particular spacing of it, in such a context as this:

The beginner who abstains as far as possible from the use of this inversion is sure therefore of being in good company. One ought, however, to add that the disfavour of the earlier masters was not shared by later composers of the Viennese and Romantic schools. Beethoven in particular has quite a partiality for the chord, which always seems to fit easily and appropriately into his harmonic scheme.

Specimens from Chapter VIII, re-worked in four parts:

B. More Extended Modulation

The addition of the fourth part entails no amplification of the text in the corresponding section of Chapter VIII. It is only matters of detail and practical workmanship that are affected.

Additional specimen from Chapter VIII, re-worked in four parts:

Chapter Twenty-Three
(Recapitulation of *Chapters Nine* and *Ten*)

TIED NOTES AND SUSPENSIONS

TIED notes and suspensions, whether plainly or ornamentally resolved, are not affected theoretically by the addition of a fourth part. So far as the text goes, therefore, a single recapitulation (and a brief one at that) will serve adequately both for Chapter IX and Chapter X. This does not imply, however, that the practical recapitulation of the exercises in four parts may be correspondingly brief; it should, on the contrary, be comprehensive and thorough.

The most important point to bear in mind is the warning, already given, that the note on which a suspension is to resolve should not be anticipated in any of the upper parts (as distinct from the bass). The effect of such anticipation is not so bad in four parts as in three, but the temptation to sin is correspondingly greater. It should be firmly resisted.

But this caution only applies in the case of downward-resolving suspensions. When the resolution is one of the upward-going semitonic kind, it may be safely and indeed advantageously anticipated by any *lower* voice. Of the following, for example, (a) is stronger in effect than (b); but (c), where the resolution is anticipated by a voice higher than the suspended part, is once more unsatisfactory; the B in the tenor, in this case, should resolve downwards (d):

There does not seem to be any discoverable reason why upward-going suspensions should differ in this particular respect from the downward-moving variety; the fact has just to be accepted as one of the many illogicalities of music.

It only remains to add a few four-part re-workings, by way of illustration, of specimens taken from Chapters IX and X:

TIED AND DOTTED NOTES

(Double suspension)

SECONDARY DIATONIC CHORDS OF THE SEVENTH (Root Position)

A. MAJOR KEYS
B. MINOR KEYS

A. *Major Keys*

IN four parts, naturally, these chords may be complete. But equally, as in the case of the dominant seventh, one note (the fifth) may be omitted, and one of the other notes doubled. The doubled note may not be the seventh; the rule against doubling an essential dissonant note holds good in any number of parts except perhaps as a very rare licence in six or eight-part writing. But either the root or the third may quite well be doubled, for the third of these secondary sevenths (unlike that of the dominant seventh, which is the leading note) is free. Here are some four-part re-workings of the examples on p. 73:

Before going further the student should give himself as much practice as may be found necessary in writing similar progressions in four parts.

Even in three-part work it appeared (see p. 73) that a seventh may conveniently resolve on to another seventh. In four-part writing, a whole chain of sevenths in sequence may thus be formed:

In the above, note particularly:

(1) The fifth is omitted from each alternate chord, the root being doubled.

(2) The third of each alternate chord remains to become the seventh of the next.

It will become apparent in the next chapter that such sequences offer interesting possibilities in the way of inversion.

B. Minor Keys

Most of what has been said above applies equally to the diatonic sevenths of the minor key. The large number of alternative forms offered by the melodic form of the scale, however, makes it advisable, once more, to add a special word of caution against doubling an essential dissonant note, or a consonant note whose progression is not free. In particular:

In II_7B Do not double the fifth.

In III_7B Do not double the fifth.

In IV_7B Do not double the third.

In VI_7B Do not double the fifth.

In VII_7B Do not double the root.

And it goes without saying that the seventh itself is still not to be doubled.

Examples from Chapter XI, re-worked in four parts:

The basses at the end of Chapter XI should now similarly be re-worked, after the preliminary exercises in preparation and resolution have received the necessary attention.

SECONDARY DIATONIC CHORDS OF THE SEVENTH (CONTINUED); THE INVERSIONS

A. FIRST INVERSIONS

B. SECOND INVERSIONS

C. THIRD INVERSIONS

D. SEQUENTIAL COMBINATIONS

A. First Inversions

THIS chord (the $^6_5$) will now normally be complete, with no doubling. The following examples (some of them re-workings from Chapter XII) mostly call for no comment; it should be noticed, however, that the first inversion of IV$_7$ (IV$_7$B in the minor) may quite well resolve (as shown) on to the first inversion of the dominant seventh:

The first inversion of the minor form I$_7$B (not recommended for three-part use) can be employed in four parts, but the bass, instead of rising a step (as usual in the resolution of a $^6_5$ chord) has to rise a fourth:

The first inversions of IV$_7$A and V$_7$A are still for the most part unsatisfactory, for the bass notes of these two chords both belong to the descending form of the scale and are therefore reluctant to proceed upwards, as the bass of a $^6_5$ should normally do. In sequence, however, other resolutions become possible, as will be shown in the final section of this chapter.

B. Second Inversions

All second inversions now become theoretically possible, alike in major and minor keys, though it will be found by experiment that some of the alternative forms—the second inversion of IV$_7$B, for example—have no satisfactory resolution and are best avoided. From now on, the student will be left to find out for himself which are the exceptions of this kind, and no attempt will be made to enumerate every possibility.

Here are more examples of the normal method of preparing and resolving these chords, both major and minor, in four parts:

It will be noticed that in practice the bass note itself is often prepared, so that the chord has the characteristic appearance of a double suspension. This is not due to any theoretical necessity: it is purely a matter of practical expediency. The choice of a suitable chord of preparation is a very limited one; in the majority of cases it happens to be a chord of which the bass note is also the bass of the ensuing $\frac{4}{3}$ chord.

C. Third Inversions

Four-part re-workings from Chapter XII:

Of the forms listed on p. 80 as being awkward either to prepare or resolve in three parts, it will be found that while some become more or less manageable in four parts, others are still recalcitrant. The method of trial and error will soon show any intelligent student whether any given form can be successfully treated in this inversion, or not.

Specimen from the end of Chapter XII, re-worked in four parts:

D. *Sequential Combinations*

It was shown in Chapter XXIV that sequential chains of diatonic sevenths in root position are quite feasible. The various inversions lend themselves admirably to similar treatment, as the following specimens will show:

The student should try his hand at similar chains, varying the keys, spacings and positions of the chords as much as possible. They should not be kept up too long; a threefold or fourfold sequence followed by a cadence either in the original or some related key will be quite enough.

He may also introduce, with advantage, a certain amount of decoration:

The realization of such four-part harmonic sequences in a two-part or three-part contrapuntal pattern is a commonplace of applied counterpoint, and the student who has practised it will find himself incomparably better prepared for the task of constructing suitable episodes and transitions in a fugue when he has reached that stage of progress.

ADDITIONAL METHODS OF MELODIC DECORATION

A. CHROMATIC UNACCENTED PASSING NOTES
B. ACCENTED PASSING AND AUXILIARY NOTES (DIATONIC)
C. ACCENTED PASSING AND AUXILIARY NOTES (CHROMATIC)

ALL these forms of decoration (and likewise those considered in Chapter XIV) are in theory unaffected by the addition of a fourth part. In practice, however, one or two hints can be given that may help to meet certain contingencies as they arise.

A. *Chromatic Unaccented Passing Notes*

It is usually better not to double the note that is altered chromatically; but a good deal depends on the spacing and relative positions of the notes thus affected. For example:

Of the above, there is no objection whatever to (a); but of the other two, (b) is certainly preferable to (c).

B. *Accented Passing and Auxiliary Notes* (*Diatonic*)

It was said in Chapter XIII (see p. 85) that the note on which an accented dissonance is to resolve may be sounded in anticipation by the bass but preferably not by an upper voice. In four-part writing, there are two common exceptions:

(1) If the dissonance resolves downwards, the note of its resolution may be anticipated in a part lying *above* the dissonance. The following, for example are very characteristic of Bach, from whom they are taken:

(2) If the dissonance resolves upwards, then the note of its resolution may advantageously be anticipated in a part lying *below* the dissonance. The following are both correct, but (b) is stronger than (a):

C. *Accented Passing and Auxiliary Notes (Chromatic)*

There is nothing special to add about these chromatic dissonances in four parts except that such 'false relations' as these are of common occurrence and add an agreeable piquancy to the sound if they are not overworked:

Note, however, in these and similar cases that the chromatically raised note must be *above* the note with which it clashes.

Here are specimen re-workings of some of the examples given in Chapter XIII:

Section A:

Section B:

Section C:

ADDITIONAL METHODS OF MELODIC DECORATION
(continued)

A. APPOGGIATURAS
B. ANTICIPATIONS
C. CHANGING NOTES

As with the embellishments described in the last chapter, so here; the addition of the extra part affects the practice to some extent, the theory not at all. And about all one can do by way of general advice is to repeat the caution against overcrowding. In particular, when the given part is itself a melody of a highly decorative character, it is a mistake (until extensive practice in four-part counterpoint has been gained) to try to do too much with the other parts; they should be content to do little more than provide the necessary harmonic support.

It only remains to give the usual specimen re-workings from Chapter XIV:

Section A:

Section B:

Section C:

Chapter Twenty-Eight

CHORDS OF THE NINTH

A. THE DOMINANT NINTH (MAJOR AND MINOR KEYS)
B. THE SECONDARY NINTHS (MAJOR AND MINOR KEYS)
C. THE SO-CALLED INVERSIONS

A. The Dominant Ninth (*Major and Minor Keys*)

Take the chord of the dominant seventh, add the ninth note from the bass on top of it, and you have, in close position, the dominant ninth in its complete form:

In four-part writing, one note of course has to be omitted, and (once more) that note is almost invariably the fifth, for the third and the seventh are essential elements of this dominant discord. The beginner is generally advised to keep the ninth as the highest note of the chord; if he follows this advice, then the normal spacings and resolution of the chord are as follows:

The position of the ninth, however, especially that of the minor ninth, may be varied without fear of producing a repellent or cacophonous effect. Such dispositions as the following will no doubt appeal less to some ears than others, but there seems no case for an absolute embargo:

The most one can honestly say is that the character of the chord is
128

markedly altered as soon as the ninth is transferred from the top floor to the first or second.

As with the dominant seventh, a submediant as well as a tonic resolution is possible. In this case, the chord of resolution is VI₇, which in turn is commonly followed by a dominant six-five, so that the whole progression is essentially cadential in character:

B. *The Secondary Ninths* (*Major and Minor Keys*)

The secondary ninths are strictly analogous, in formation, to the dominant ninth, to which they are related exactly as the secondary sevenths are to the dominant seventh. In the case of the dominant, that is to say, both seventh and ninth may be approached freely; in that of the secondaries, both are better if prepared. And there is a stronger case, so far as the secondaries are concerned, for insisting that the ninth should be kept as the highest note of the chord. It will be found by experiment that (in the minor key especially) many of these theoretically possible chords are awkward or impracticable when it comes to the point of using them. The fact that two of the notes in the chord have to be prepared is a severely limiting factor, and for this reason alone—apart from possible difficulties of resolution—the suitable occasions for employing these secondary ninths will be found in practice to occur very seldom. Here are a few examples:

The student may try a few similar progressions (in other keys) for himself, including both dominant and secondary types. To set specially contrived exercises calling for the introduction of these chords at specified points would clearly be futile.

Figuring. ⁹⁄₇ is the normal figuring.

C. *The So-called Inversions*

It will be noticed that in the chapter-heading reference is made to the 'so-called' inversions of the ninth. This epithet calls for a word of explanation.

Consider such chords as the following:

These are generally felt to be unsatisfactory, because the note on which one of the dissonant notes, (the ninth of the chord in its root position) is about to resolve is now already present in one of the upper parts, and we have already learnt that this kind of anticipation is best avoided. The proper and natural course, therefore, is to say simply that the inversions of the ninth are not used.

There are those, however, who prefer to say that the inversions *can* be used, provided the root is omitted. But in that case the 'inversions' become identical with the diatonic chords of the seventh, so that no further explanation of them is required.

It seems to the author, moreover, that a chord from which the root has to be omitted ceases *ipso facto* to be that chord at all, and that no support should be given to so paradoxical a method of classification.

Chapter Twenty-Nine

THE HARMONIZATION OF CHORALES

THE harmonization of chorales is admittedly a special branch of the art. Yet no serious student of harmony can afford to neglect it, because it is from this and this only that he can obtain, by practice, a direct and detailed understanding of Bach's harmonic principles and methods. Bach, when all is said and done, is the father of harmony, and his chorale settings provide an unsurpassable corpus of harmonic study, unmatched alike for technical resource and for profundity of emotional utterance. No other worker in the same field has produced anything even remotely comparable to his stupendous achievement.[1]

The prime essential, needless to say, is first-hand study of the settings themselves. The remainder of this chapter consists merely of a few pointers intended—perhaps too optimistically—to facilitate and clarify that study.

First of all, a word about the actual tunes. Many if not most of these date back to the sixteenth century and are modal in structure. It is not proposed here to give a dissertation on the modal system; those who wish to learn about it should consult the proper authorities, such as *Grove's Dictionary* or the *Oxford History of Music*. It may be helpful, however, to say just this much—that two of the modes most commonly found in use are the Dorian and the Phrygian. There are also Mixolydian examples, but they are few and far between. Those unfamiliar with the modes may distinguish these by the following rule of thumb:

Dorian, will appear as minor tunes with one sharp too many or one flat too few in the signature.

Phrygian, will also appear as minor tunes, but with one flat too many or one sharp too few in the signature.

Mixolydian, will appear as major tunes, but with one sharp too few or one flat too many in the signature.

The other modes—Lydian, Ionian, Aeolian—may be considered for the present purpose as equivalent to our own major (Lydian and Ionian) and minor (Aeolian).

Bach does not attempt to harmonize these tunes in any archaic 'modal' fashion; he applies to all alike his own free methods of harmony and modulation. It will often be found, however, that the Dorian, Phrygian and Mixolydian settings will, to an inexperienced ear, sound 'out of the

---

[1] The best editions for study are those of B. F. Richter (Breitkopf and Haertel). H. Elliot Button (Novello), and C. Sanford Terry (Oxford University Press). All these collections are practically complete, and all are so arranged that Bach's different settings of the same tune (where such exist) are grouped together. The facility for comparative study thus afforded is of the utmost value.

key' at the finish; that is to say, the final cadence will suggest the dominant or sub-dominant rather than the tonic chord. That impression will gradually pass away as familiarity grows.

Let us now pass very briefly in review certain features of these settings to which it seems advisable to draw particular attention. To save quoting long German titles, the references for the examples are given by numbers which indicate the number of the setting in the Breitkopf edition. The figures in brackets indicate the bar numbers, reckoning from the first *complete* bar of the chorale.

(1) *Syllabication*. All voices have to sing the same number of syllables. Where notes in the tune are slurred, those notes are sung to one syllable, and may be harmonized to a single note in all or any of the other parts. Apart from this, every note in the tune will require a note (or two or more slurred notes) in each of the other voices. Therefore, if it is desired for any voice to sing the same note on two successive beats, two crotchets will have to be used, not a minim.

(2) *Ornamentation of tunes*. The tunes are mostly more or less plain—plain at any rate in comparison with the floriated arabesques into which they are transformed in some of the chorale preludes. But occasional ornaments—passing notes, anticipatory notes and so forth—are frequently introduced. Compare for instance these versions of 244 (12, 13) and 242 (12, 13), the latter being transposed from E flat to D to facilitate the comparison:

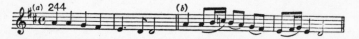

The chorales given as exercises at the end of the chapter are, with hardly an exception, set down in plain notes; the student should consider himself free to introduce occasional ornamental notes in the manner above indicated, should he so desire, especially when re-working a tune for the second or third time.

(3) *Texture*. There is a good deal of variety here. At the one extreme are such settings as 9, 68, 81, and 327, which are almost entirely note against note settings; at the other, contrast with them (e.g.) 225 and 349, where the texture approximates more to that of the simpler chorale preludes. Most of the settings lie midway between these two extremes, and it is these which the student should take, in the first place, as his models.

It will be noticed that in order to facilitate the flow of the parts and make them individually interesting, Bach does not boggle at occasional abnormalities of spacing and distribution, crossing and overlapping of parts, and so forth. It is also worth observing (and it very seldom *is* observed) that although he uses accented passing dissonances with the utmost boldness and freedom, he yet abstains almost entirely from the genuine appoggiatura. For example, he will make a point of writing

in preference to

(4) *Cadence.* Bach's treatment of the leading note in a perfect cadence calls for comment. When the leading note in the penultimate chord is in either of the middle voices, and one of the voices above it then moves to the tonic, the leading note commonly moves down to the fifth, instead of pursuing its natural course—as it is generally considered—up to the tonic. Few would regard this as good counterpoint; but Bach was evidently prepared to let this convention go by the board in order to obtain a full four-part chord for his close. Those who feel that more is lost than gained by this procedure are in no wise bound to follow his example.

He also quite frequently takes his leading note up to the mediant, even in a minor key, when the leap involved is that of a diminished fourth, and that in places where a more orthodox cadential formation could easily have been contrived. Even such cadential eccentricities as the following are to be found:

More will be said later about Bach's general attitude to harmonic licence, of which the above cadences may certainly serve as examples.

In quite a different category is a cadence like this:

In the above, it is precisely the unexpected deviation into D major, with the fall of the C sharp (now become the leading note) to the fifth of the new tonic chord, that gives the cadence its peculiar charm. It is not very uncommon for one line of the tune to end thus, and when it does so, Bach usually prefers an orthodox cadence in the relative minor. He knew quite well that the effectiveness of such unexpected turns varies inversely as their frequency.

(5) *Consecutives*. In the matter of prohibited consecutives Bach is strict, but not pedantic. He accepts the working rule first established by sixteenth-century practice that there is no objection to consecutives on successive beats provided a subsidiary harmony note is introduced between them, e.g.:

It is greatly to be hoped that examiners who set a chorale melody or bass to be harmonized 'in the style of J. S. Bach' (as they are fond of doing) will take the trouble to acquaint themselves with Bach's attitude to this question. Many of them at present seem to be unaware of it.

The use of what might be called a 'subsidiary seventh' in the bass for a similar purpose is another device frequently adopted by Bach in situations like the following:

It has already been observed in Chapter IX that consecutive fifths interrupted by a suspension are frowned upon by examiners but accepted by all reputable composers. Bach is no exception:

Nor was he prepared to take too serious a view of anticipatory notes:

(6) It should be understood that although these settings are genuine examples of pure vocal counterpoint, yet in practice the parts were doubled at performance by the organ, so that the bass was doubled in the lower octave by the sixteen-foot coupler. Such apparent solecisms as this are therefore not what they seem:

(7) *Licences in general.* Samuel Butler remarks somewhere (in the *Notebooks*, if memory serves) that whereas Handel in general keeps to the rules but takes a good thumping licence every now and again when he feels inclined, Bach is taking little niggling licences the whole time. Butler's musical judgements have only a comic value, yet in this particular matter there is an element of truth in what he says. Bach *does* allow his parts great freedom of movement; so much will already have been gathered from what has been said in this chapter. The watchful reader will find many other seeming departures from the path of orthodoxy, though in truth they are not so many when viewed in relation to the enormous volume of Bach's output in this and other fields. The student is not called upon to outdo Bach in this respect; but he will find it interesting and instructive, when he comes across such a passage, to pause and consider whether he can see any definite reason why Bach should have written just so and not otherwise, and whether the licentious element could be eliminated without a too drastic reconstruction of the passage as a whole.

It was not easy to select, from so vast a corpus, one or two that might serve as illustrations to the foregoing remarks. The two finally chosen— No. 262 ('Nun Freut euch, lieben Christen g'mein') and 342 ('Was mein Gott will')—were not picked out because they are specially simple, or specially elaborate, or specially well known, or specially anything else, but simply because they are beautiful and at the same time absolutely typical specimens of Bach's normal method. As such they seem, in the light of what has already been said about that method, to call for no detailed comment.

Appended for the sake of convenience are eighteen chorales, in various keys and modes, for the student to work upon. They are set down here in their simplest form; it has already been suggested that a limited amount of decorative variation may be introduced at discretion. And it cannot be too strongly recommended that each tune should be harmonized in several ways—three or four at least—and that the student should make it a rule, after choosing one tune to work on, not to pass on to another until he feels sure that he has explored every reasonable possibility offered by the one selected. While some variety in the texture of the different versions is naturally permissible, the object is by no means to make each setting more elaborate than the one before, but to make all of them, as music, equally convincing.

A. *Major:*

B. *Minor:*

8. Minor

Herr, ich habe missgehandelt

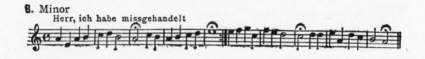

Herzliebster Jesu

Jesu, der du meine Seele

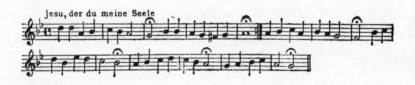

Keinen hat Gott verlassen

Sei gegrüsset

Christ, der du bist

C. *Modal:*

C. Modal

Gelobet seist du

Komm, Gott Schöpfer

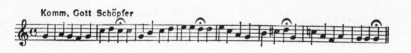

Erschienen ist der herrlisch' Tag

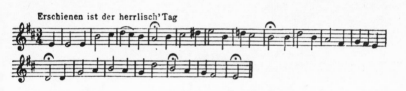

Vater unser

Aus tiefer Noth

Erbarm' dich mein

Printed in
Great Britain
by
Ebenezer Baylis and Son Ltd
Worcester and London